MORE TALES OF A BOMBER COMMAND WAAF

First edition, published in 2003 by

WOODFIELD PUBLISHING
Woodfield House, Babsham Lane, Bognor Regis
West Sussex PO21 5EL, England.

ISBN 1-903953-46-4

Cover photograph: The Author with Bridget's son Redwine, aged 2.

More Tales of a
Bomber Command WAAF
(and her horse)

SYLVIA (BUNTY) PICKERING

Woodfield

*Dedicated to the memory of the 104,000 Bomber Command
Aircrew who operated during World War II,
particularly those of No. 5 Group.*

They were my heroes when I was eighteen.

They are still my heroes now that I am over eighty.

Killed in action or died as POW.s	*47,268*
Killed in flying or ground accidents	*8,195*
Killed in ground battle action	*37*
Total fatalities	*55,500*
POW's	*9,838*
Injured/wounded other than POW's	*8,403*

*All author's royalties from the sale of this book
will be donated to RAF charities.*

Tales of a Bomber Command Waaf (and her horse)

Sylvia Pickering • 2002

ISBN 1-903953-24-3 • £9.95+£1.50 p&p

In January 1941 Sylvia Pickering eagerly set off for No.1 WAAF Reception Centre at the Grand Hotel, Harrogate, leaving behind her sheltered home life in rural Lincolnshire to join other young volunteers – some of whom had travelled from as far away as Australia and New Zealand – to pull together and 'do their bit' to save Great Britain from imminent danger and invasion.

Thanks to Sylvia's rediscovery of some long-stored letters, both written and received by herself, we have the opportunity to peep into the world of a generation of young people who left home early and had to grow up quickly, learning about life and love against the backdrop of a world at war.

Sylvia's story takes place in the 'bomber county' of Lincolnshire, where so many of RAF Bomber Command's wartime aerodromes were situated, and we follow her on active duty to the Armoury at RAF Cottesmore and Station Sick Quarters at RAF Coningsby.

In her letters, the voice of Sylvia's youthful self describes such diverse off-duty pursuits as learning to dance the tango, visits to the cinema and horse-riding on her beloved mare, Bridget. (Somewhat unusually, her horse accompanied her wherever she went during the war.) We also discover her views on the potency of pink gin, the problems of transport in the blackout, and of course the joys and heartbreaks of her inevitable romantic entanglements, in particular her relationship with a young Australian airman with whom she lost touch, as was so often the case in those days, when he was posted elsewhere. It was to be 50 years before she discovered what had happened to him…

Although Sylvia modestly describes her book as a 'perfectly ordinary story' of a WAAF at war, it constitutes a very worthwhile piece of social history. As Dr Tessa Stone of Newnham College, Cambridge writes in her foreword: "it is a chronicle of some of the extraordinary people who did extraordinary things at an extraordinary time."

AVAILABLE DIRECT FROM THE PUBLISHERS
WOODFIELD PUBLISHING • BOGNOR REGIS • WEST SUSSEX • PO21 5EL
telephone 01243 821234 • ww.woodfieldpublishing.com

Contents

ACKNOWLEDGEMENTS

First and last I wish to thank Dawn Bowskill for freely giving of her time and skill with a computer in order to make it possible for my two books to be compiled so successfully. Also, to Colin, her husband, for his ability to improve so dramatically some very old photos of mine.

There are four people whom I particularly wish to thank, as they have helped me with both my books. Once again Dr Tessa Stone has offered to find time in order to write a most generous Foreword. John Larder has provided concise details of the work of 5 Group Bomber Command. Ted Richardson let me have the full details of Tom's ops from the Operational Record Book of 463 R.A.A.F. Squadron. Norman Small in Australia managed to contact Ken's sister for me so I have been able to include a photograph of Ken and his lovely wife.

In Chapter One is a depressing photo of Morton Hall, lent to me by Lyn Saunders who is the Governor of the Womens' Prison which is now on the site.

I am glad to include a photo of the River Witham which appears in Chapter Eleven taken by Beryl Commin on a visit to us. This clearly shows where we walked so unsteadily on that memorable night and that now there is wire netting instead of two widely spaced bars preventing easy access to the murky waters below!

I am grateful to Fred Stead, Secretary of the Air Gunners' Association, for providing in Chapter Fifteen, graphic details of Tom's P.O.W. imprisonment and forced march under really horrific conditions. My thanks go to Jenny Toyne for providing the maps.

Finally I wish to thank Nick and Linda Shepperd of Wood-field Publishing for the fine quality of the books they have produced for me. I think the design and subject for the covers is both attractive and unexpected.

It is almost three years since Dawn and I first met and now we are busy finalising the second book we have produced. On so many Tuesday mornings I would walk along to her house and we would spend the morning either discussing and putting into her computer the work I had produced the previous week on my elderly typewriter. Alternatively, painstakingly and patiently changing words here and there as I changed my mind about the exact words to use! My everlasting thanks to Dawn for enabling me to have published the true story of five years of my life spent as a volunteer in the WAAF in WWII.

It is a great delight and honour to introduce the second volume of Sylvia's memoirs of her service in the WAAF, and to be plunged vividly once again into a world where 'irons', 'biscuits', 'drill' and 'scrambled egg' had a very different meaning to those ascribed to them today.

We pick up Sylvia's trail when she is posted away from Coningsby in disgrace, as a 'disturbing influence' and 'subversive element', only to prove her detractors wrong in the most satisfying possible way at her new station. We follow her progress as a Non-Commissioned Officer winning over difficult colleagues, and the ebb and flow of her complicated social life, including the wonderful tale of an evening spent getting drunk, just to find out what others 'found so enjoyable' about the process!

We also meet a new cast of characters, including two Australians - Rear Gunner Tom Whiteley, and Mid-Upper Gunner Ken – whose gentle competition for Sylvia's affections are charted in Ken's playful, hopeful letters. Indeed, it is refreshing in an age when written communication is dominated by a cursory email to be reminded of the importance of letters during wartime, and the frequency with which people wrote; astonishing to someone of my generation. It is thus a great privilege to be able to read the letters from Jimmy, Sylvia's fiancé; remarkable, eloquent love letters of the sort which, one regrettably suspects, feature less and less in modern relationships.

In this volume as in the previous one Sylvia's personal journey through the WAAF is skilfully and sensitively placed in the broader context of war, and through her research into

Tom Whiteley's experiences as a Prisoner of War in Stalag Luft 7 we are reminded of some of the dreadful privations faced by those who fought. We are also reminded of what they were fighting for, however: the peace which saw Sylvia finally able to indulge her passion for horses, find happiness in her marriage, and, at the age of eighty, publish her second, remarkable book. I sincerely hope that others will be inspired by the pages that follow to take up Sylvia's challenge, and 'put down what life was like for you … and let your thoughts and feelings be handed down' to future generations.

Dr Tessa Stone
Kingston Upon Thames

In my previous book, Tales of a Bomber Command WAAF and her Horse, I describe what life was like for me from my enlistment on 1st January, 1941 to November 1943 after postings to R.A.F. Cottesmore and R.A.F. Coningsby. Now, in this book, I tell of my final posting to H.Q. 5 Group (Bomber Command) at R.A.F. Morton Hall, near Swinderby in Lincolnshire where I remained until my demob on 8th January, 1946.

I have tried to give a feeling of what daily life was like and how I felt in those far off days before most of my readers were born.

After my demob. I never gave a thought to my time in the WAAF until VE day + 50 years took place in 1995 when press coverage reminded my of those days and I realised how dramatically life had changed since then. During a feeling of nostalgia I wrote some little stories about events which had occurred to me. I wondered what had happened to my close friends after the war and the final chapters of this book entitled "50 Years On" tells of what I found.

It was only in 1997 that I rediscovered treasured letters which had lain stowed away since the 1950's. It was an incredible feeling to read them once again after a gap of so many years since they were written. Those from Jimmy touch me greatly, as I think they are wonderful because they were written with such depth of feeling.

I know there are people who would consider that such personal letters should not be published. I have thought the matter over long and carefully. I have come to the opposite conclusion. What is the point of treasuring these letters for sixty years and then for them to be thrown away like unwanted junk mail? Here are rare examples of letters written in wartime describing genuine feelings held at that time by those who wrote the letters. Those letters from Jimmy very well illustrate how it is actually possible to meet someone, fall in love, become engaged, hire a wedding dress and part – never to meet again – in well under a year. I had always imagined that such behaviour only happened to very flighty people – how wrong I was!

I still have very clear memories of those special friends who were such a part of my life in those dangerous days when we were all young. I am happy to share them with you.

In wartime I used to eagerly await the arrival of letters from friends. Now, sixty years later, I still scan the post with enthusiasm for I now hope to find a letter from someone who wishes to buy a copy of one of my books.

My first book was published in mid November 2002. Five months later I am delighted to report that profits from its sale have enabled me to donate £500 to the Air Crew Association. Also, a cheque for £250 will shortly be given to Thorp Camp Preservation Group which is restoring part of the camp site of R.A.F. Woodhall Spa which is where my friend Roo was stationed in the Autumn of 1942. A Visitor Centre has been created there and last year four memorials were built in memory of the squadrons who were based there during WW II. The £250 will help pay for the centrepiece of a propeller to be installed on a brick plinth.

All future profits from my books will be donated similarly.

Sylvia Pickering
July, 2003

Location Map showing Sylvia's three postings[1]

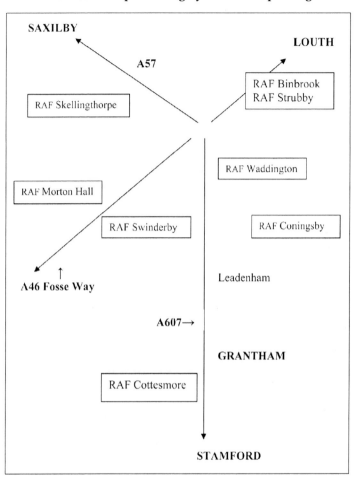

1. *Headquarters No. 5 Group Bomber Command*

In my first book I told how I volunteered to join the WAAF and was enlisted at No. 1 WAAF Depot, at the Grand Hotel, Harrogate, in that snow encrusted town, on 1st January, 1941. This was followed by two very happy years as the clerk of the Station Armament Officer at 14 O.T.U. R.A.F. Cottesmore in Rutland; my traumatic time at home on compassionate leave to nurse my dying mother after which I was posted as clerk to the Senior Medical Officer at R.A.F. Coningsby in Lincolnshire where I spent a very unhappy nine months.

Sadly the S.M.O. considered me to be a "disturbing influence" and a "subversive element". I was suddenly informed that I was to "get cleared" as I had been posted to H.Q. 5 Group (Bomber Command) at Morton Hall, Swinderby, eight miles south-west of Lincoln, in exchange for another clerk. I was delighted to be leaving S.S.Q. at Coningsby but wondered very much what sort of a reception should I receive at Morton Hall? Had this girl wished to leave Morton Hall as much as I wished to leave Coningsby? All would soon be revealed in a way I had not expected.

Life at a Group H.Q. would be vastly different from my previous postings to R.A.F. Cottesmore and R.A.F. Coningsby where the vast expanse of grassy airfield was dominated on the skyline by huge hangars and men and women of numerous trades were busy round and about preparing either for training flights or bombing raids and there was usually the noise of aircraft engines either in the sky or on the ground. Numbers at Group were relatively small as most people worked in offices with appropriate Messing and Admin staff to cater for their needs.

In point of fact I was very privileged to have a posting to 5 Group H.Q. as it was regarded as one of the finest, if not the finest Group in Bomber Command, and aircraft from the Group were capable of making raids on the enemy only needing to use aircraft from 5 Group as they even supplied their own Pathfinder Force. I asked John Larder to give me some facts about 5 Group and this is what he wrote:

The group had been led by Alec Coryton in its formative time, who fell out with Harris and was sacked. He was succeeded by Ralph Cochrane in February 1943 who although lacking operational experience had the ear of Harris and was a demanding and successful commander. Coryton had objected to the loss of 83 Squadron to 8 Group and ironically it was his successor who recovered 83 and 97 Squadrons as well as getting 627 Squadron with its Mosquitoes to lead the Group's own Pathfinder Force. The Group was in the forefront of operations from 1942 when it took part in the first "1000 bomber" raids, the Augsburg daylight raid, the "Dams" Raid, the "Noball" campaign against the V-weapons successfully carried out by 617 Squadron, Mailly le Camp and the attacks on oil and transportation. Tactically it led in low level marking and the introduction of the master bomber. Many of its members not only earned decorations but rose to high rank throughout the R.A.F.

The Headquarters of 5 Group had been located in a large house in Grantham called St. Vincents, however, in November, 1943 it was moved to Morton Hall, a large brick built house standing in fine park-like grounds studded with a wide range of unusual and handsome trees which in 1933 was owned by Mr H. G. Torr. This move of H.Q. 5 Group necessitated another move for 5 Group Commando School which had transferred in March 1943 to R.A.F. Morton Hall. The purpose of the Commando School was to physically toughen up 5 Group aircrew and teach them evasion techniques in case they should be shot down over enemy territory.

An undated photo of a sad and lifeless Morton Hall probably taken
after it had been vacated by H.Q. 5 Group (Bomber Command).
(Reproduced by kind permission of the Governor of HM Prison Morton Hall.)

The final part of their training took place at the Heavy Conversion Unit nearby at R.A.F. Swinderby. This School was transferred to R.A.F. Scampton at a time when there were no squadrons there as concrete runways were being built which were needed to carry the increased weight of the much heavier four engined Stirlings and Lancasters which were now being used. However, at this time R.A.F. Scampton still remained as H.Q. 52 Base Station and controlled the two satellite stations of R.A.F. Fiskerton and R.A.F. Dunholme Lodge. When I was posted to R.A.F. Coningsby in the Spring of 1943 I believe that 5 Group consisted of fifteen R.A.F. Stations as follows:

BASE STATIONS:	SATELLITES:
WADDINGTON –	Bardney and Faldingworth
EAST KIRKBY –	Spilsby and Strubby
SCAMPTON –	Dunholme Lodge and Fiskerton
CONINSGBY –	Woodhall Spa and Metheringham
SWINDERBY –	Skellingthorpe and Wigsley

Later on Scampton and Wigsley were moved out of 5 Group. We also had our own Heavy Conversion Unit which was at R.A.F. Swinderby.

I arrived at Morton Hall very shortly after the move from St. Vincents had taken place. I was allocated a table at the side of a very large room, probably a temporary Orderly Room, filled with clerks. In the wall beside my table was a small hatch similar to those seen between dining rooms and kitchens – on the other side of which was where my two bosses, Lt. Col. Frank Russell and S/Ldr. Philip T. Bowcock, had their own office. They were the two Group Defence Officers responsible for the defence of all airfields and landing grounds in 5 Group from any attack by the enemy.

It was immediately made obvious that the girl with whom I had had an "exchange posting" had not wished to be posted from Group to make room for me; her friends were very upset about it and I was made the target for their anger. I was "sent to Coventry" by my fellow clerks. My posting was indeed a case of "out of the frying pan" of Coningsby "into the fire" of Group.

Although I can well understand why the other WAAF clerks were upset that I had unwittingly been the cause of their friend being posted in my place, nevertheless I cannot help feeling that if this girl had been more diligent in attending to her duties, her bosses at Group would not have let her go in order to receive in exchange "a subversive element" and "a Bolshie" as I had been labelled by the S.M.O. at R.A.F. Coningsby. Fortunately, for my sake, there was one clerk who befriended me. Her name was Beryl Commin and she worked with three others in 'P' staff who were responsible for maintaining aircrew at maximum strength throughout 5 Group and matters relating to discipline in crews. They were often requested to move somebody off squadron within hours if they did not fit in or were not up to standard. We often used to go out together and are still in close contact. I hate to think what life would have been like for me without her friendship. Beryl has since told me that unlike other postings, it was most unusual for anyone to be posted from Group H.Q. once they had settled in there. Consequently this must have been an unexpected, nasty shock for the girl to be posted away from Group to take my place at Coningsby.

Thankfully my bosses and I were very soon given our own offices at the top of the Hall which we reached by ascending the steep wooden servants' staircases at the back of the building.

My bosses had a spacious airy room on the second floor on the left of the picture of Morton Hall with a large window beneath the slated roof. I had a small room off it lit by a skylight. The two H.Q. 5 Group Photographic Officers also had an office on this floor and I occasionally did some typing for these very pleasant gentlemen.

It was very peaceful up there, as no one else used those staircases. Even now, I can remember how I always had advance warning of when the Colonel was returning to his eyrie at the top of the building. When he started up the last flight of uncarpeted wooden stairs his heavy tread – and even heavier breathing – gave early warning of his coming, long before he actually appeared in the rather narrow doorway. In retrospect there were delightful similarities between the Colonel and Captain Mainwaring of that excellent television series "Dad's Army". They were both middle aged, bespectacled, with small moustaches, solidly built and not very fit. I now no longer saw the other clerks in the large office and peace reigned once more as far as my office life was concerned and again I was happy in my work.

2. *Life At Morton Hall*

When I was at R.A.F. Cottesmore the WAAFs were billeted well away from the airfield in large private houses in case the airfield was attacked. At R.A.F. Coningsby, when not on night duty in Station Sick Quarters, I slept in a Nissen hut on the far side of the village adjacent to the B1192 (the road to Boston) about two miles away – in a field which is now covered by houses. So it was a delight to find that at Group all the WAAFs slept in Nissen "tin huts" in a grassy paddock near to the Hall itself. This meant that it was not far to walk to the Mess for breakfast and after the mid-day meal I could go back to wash in the Ablution Block and freshen up in the hut before returning to the office for the afternoon's work.

I think there were about fourteen or fifteen girls usually of the same trade in a hut. There was an odd number because a small section at one end of the hut was normally partitioned off for the sole use of the N.C.O. in charge of that particular hut but not all huts had an N.C.O. in charge, so some huts did not have this separate space.

Our furniture consisted of a green painted metal cupboard in which we could hang our greatcoat, No. 1 "best" jacket and skirt and keep our cap and shoes. This cupboard was not lockable. Latterly we were each given "a bomb box" which had a metal hasp through which one could thread a padlock so, at last, one had somewhere safe in which to keep one's bits and pieces. It was just wide enough to keep a clean shirt in when it was still neatly folded as returned from the laundry; a limited amount of which was usually permitted to be sent out once a week. The bomb box was also just low enough so that it could be slid underneath one's metal bedstead out of sight. At each end of the box was a twisted wire handle covered with leather, its original use was probably to carry 11lb practice smoke bombs and the box weighed 16lbs when empty. Mine is on display at the Aviation Heritage Centre at East Kirkby in Lincolnshire. I seem to remember that quite high up on the wall a long narrow shelf ran along the whole length of the hut where photos and other small personal treasures could be displayed. There were no chairs so we had to use our beds to sit on when polishing buttons etc. This was a daily chore as both jacket and greatcoat, as well as the cap badge, were made of brass and tarnished very quickly particularly in damp or wintry weather.

When I was initially kitted out at Harrogate I was issued with two jackets and skirts, one greatcoat for winter use and a cap and cap badge. Illogical as it may seem I believe there was a rule that greatcoats must not be worn before a given date in the Autumn no matter what the weather was like! One jacket and skirt was specially kept for parades and for going out when off duty and it was known as Best Blues or our No. 1 uniform. The other was for daily use when on duty, however, it was not necessary to change into Best Blues for fortnightly Pay Parades for then one merely lined up in a building and pay was handed out in alphabetical order. When one's name was called out you marched up to the pay officer, saluted, called out the last three digits of your Service number and after picking up your pay returned immediately to duty.

We always liked to look our best when going off duty particularly if leaving camp when one usually chose to wear Best Blues, a freshly ironed clean shirt and, if possible, a smart good-looking Van Heusen collar as those issued to us were always very limp unless starched. It was difficult to obtain Van Heusen collars as clothing coupons were needed for them.

On leaving the office after the day's work it was straight to the Mess for our third and final meal of the day there – a sort of "high tea". Then back to our nearby huts to change into our "Best Blues" after making sure buttons, cap badge and shoes were well polished. I had a favourite pair of low heeled black uniform shoes which polished up well and which I used to prefer to wear when going to a dance.

For buttons and cap badge Brasso metal polish or the impregnated cotton wool Duraglit was usually used, although Silvo was preferred by some as they thought it gave a pleasant silvery sheen to the buttons rather than such a brassy look. A metal button-stick was slid behind the buttons when cleaning them to keep the metal polish off the material. Our serviceable but heavy grey lisle stockings were worn inside out by some girls when going off camp thinking they looked better that way, however, if caught by the Service Police they ran the risk of being put on a charge for wearing the King's uniform incorrectly – or words to that effect!

After a time WAAFs in such trades as drivers, balloon operators and parachute packers were issued with the much more comfortable battle dress to wear – a loose fitting blue blouson type jacket and trousers – which had NO BRASS BUTTONS to clean! As a clerk, I always had to wear a uniform jacket and skirt. I have recently seen WAAFs on R.A.F. Waddington camp going about in big woollen jumpers over their shirts, collars and ties instead of a jacket and so they do not appear to have ANY buttons to polish – lucky girls.

Kit inspections were the bane of my life; fortunately for me they were only held infrequently. I do not remember ever being able to lay out on my bed ready for inspection a full set of kit to prove that all the items which the R.A.F. had lent me were still safely in my possession. I think I rarely lost items through carelessness but that when the date of a kit inspection was announced items which others had lost were "'alf-inched" from those who still had that particular item. As the Inspecting WAAF Officer NEVER looked at the name on the garment displayed to see if it matched that person's display of kit the true position was never revealed. Here is an example of deficiencies of my kit at an inspection on 26th October, 1942 when I was stationed at R.A.F. Cottesmore.

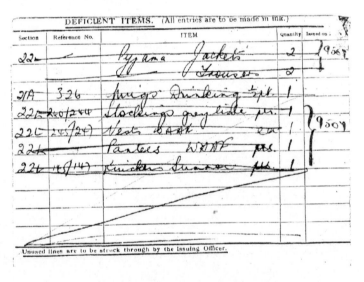

Second part Kit Inspection Deficiencies.

It is followed by an R.A.F. Form 1383 issued when I was at Morton Hall dated 14th June, 1944 stating that we were to be issued with navy blue shoulder bags. I hardly used it at all before it disappeared beyond recall!

Form 1383 for additional kit to be issued.

Kit Parades were held about once a month over at the Equipment Section. There one could exchange a worn-out issued garment for a new one. On the rare occasions when a jacket, great coat or cap had to be exchanged, one always tried to keep the old set of buttons and the cap badge to put on the replacement garment. For, after several hundred polishings, they were worn much smoother and could be made to shine quite brilliantly. New buttons might indicate that you were a new recruit to the WAAF – we all wanted to look as if we had "got some in" (service that is) and that we were old-timers in the Service and not "sprogs" or newcomers.

I usually obtained my make-up from the NAAFI; news quickly spread when it was heard that "the NAFFI had got some make-up in". I don't remember much choice – although I can clearly remember the name of 'Californian Poppy' perfume – but it was sensibly rationed as was the case when any confectionery arrived there.

On the springs of our metal bedstead each night we laid out three square solid mattresses, which I believe were filled with tightly packed straw and were called "biscuits". Being WAAFs we had the luxury of a tough pair of unbleached cotton drill sheets and similar material was made into a sort of bolster shape to cover our very solid "pillow" and it had tapes at the end to keep the alliance together. I think we had four dark coloured blankets issued to each of us. (After the War there was a glut of these blankets on the market for use as under rugs for horses in stables at about 10/-[1] each, but I never considered them suitable for any horses in my charge as I knew, from personal experience, that it was difficult to keep warm beneath them.)

Before going to breakfast we had to "stack our beds". The three biscuits were stacked on top of each other at the head of the bed. All the sheets and blankets, except one, were folded up neatly and placed alternately on top of each other with the rounded fold facing towards the bottom of the bed. The other blanket was folded into four lengthways and wrapped neatly around the bundle of sheets and blankets and placed on top of the biscuits with the pillow resting

----

[1] 50 new pence

proudly on top of everything. Beds remained stacked until the evening when one came off duty and they were usually made up before going out in the evening as there was quite a knack in getting the rather meagre blankets to retain the biscuit at the foot of the bed to stay on the metal bedstead. So it was easier to make up one's bed with the hut lights on rather than trying to do it in darkness if one came in late after "lights out".

Nowadays one is so accustomed to living in a dwelling warmed by some form of central heating that it must be hard to appreciate that the only warmth came from a little cast iron stove in the middle of the hut whose chimney poked through the tin roof above. Daily we had to light it, feed it with our ration of coke and clean it out afterwards and dispose of the ashes. Those on day duty were not permitted to light it before 5 p.m. – even if the weather was freezing or snowing. I cannot remember if the rules were relaxed for those who were on shift work. Needless to say we were always on the look-out for any "unofficial" opportunities to acquire extra coke to augment our "official" supply.

The floor covering was linoleum laid loosely over the concrete floor of the hut. The most prized bed-spaces were those nearest to the stove in the middle of the hut – even if one did have some disturbance in cold weather from girls trying to boil water on it in order to make a hot drink, fill a hot water bottle, make toast or thaw themselves out and sitting on the end of your bed in order to do so.

Those whose bedspace was furthest from the warmth of the stove often had to contend with a damp bed-space, as moisture from the concrete floor came up through the linoleum and remained on the surface as fine bubbles – making it quite impossible to buff up that part of the hut into a really shiny surface ready for the WAAF Officer's inspection. It was always "Camp Night" once a week when we were not allowed out but expected to attend to any necessary domestic chores followed up by a thorough cleaning and polishing of our quarters – wielding the heavy "floor bumper" or polisher (which was heavily weighted) with vigour ready for inspection the following day after we had gone to attend to our various duties. In due course a list of huts with the Inspecting Officer's remarks was pinned up, with comments varying from 'very good indeed' (rare) to 'disgraceful' or some such epithet.

In the days before indoor lavatories were commonplace our parents had a chamber pot beneath the bed which they could use in the privacy and comparative warmth of the bedroom. Imagine what it was like for us. We had reluctantly to prise our way out from beneath harsh sheets and hairy blankets wearing Service issue striped flannelette pyjamas,[1] put on one's greatcoat (which in winter was usually spread over the bed for extra warmth), push bare feet into cold leather Service shoes and either follow the path in the darkness to the Ablution Block or take a short cut across the wet or frozen grass, and risk getting one's already "cleaned for the morning" shoes wet or muddy.

The Ablution block was in the middle of the paddock and thoroughly blacked out. It was rather dimly lit inside by a blue painted electric light bulb and contained ironing facilities as well as wash basins, lavatories and bathrooms. The floors, once again, were concrete and liberally supplied with wooden slatted boards (known as duck-boards)[2] on which to

---

[1] or our own night attire if coupons made that possible

[2] it amuses me to see that these are now advertised for sale as "fashionable
>>>

stand as, more often than not, the floors were very wet – and cold.

We did quite a lot of washing in the Ablution Block and, in order to save fuel, bath water was not supposed to be more than six inches deep. However, we could not wash either ourselves or our clothes unless we remembered to take with us a plug for the wash basin or bath. It really is incredible that, throughout the Royal Air Force, it was rare to find a wash basin or bath that had a plug in it. No doubt every basin or bath had a plug to begin with when they were installed, so, who took them in the first place? An unsolved mystery of the Second World War!

The food at Group H.Q. was wonderful. For example, at our mid-day meal there was always a choice of three hot and two cold main dishes. Beryl says that our chef was from the Trocadero Restaurant in London – tall, dark and quite handsome.

One day I had been working late in the office and by the time I arrived at the Mess little choice remained. I was offered a plateful of something which I thought was a type of pasta or spaghetti in a milky sauce. It was really quite pleasant and I ate it all up with relish. It was only later when I discovered that I had been eating TRIPE that my gorge rose within me! Isn't it amazing how our mind can so greatly influence our taste buds? I have always disliked eating what I called "innards" – liver, kidney, heart, brains and every sort of offal. As my father so rightly used to say to me "If you were as nice as you are particular...!"

---

bathroom accessories" for modern homes albeit of a more attractive design than those we used!

A half pint earthenware mug, a knife, fork and a spoon were issued to us and known as our "irons". If we wanted to eat or drink it was necessary to take our "irons" with us. On leaving the Mess we passed a huge tank of supposedly boiling water into which we took our turn to dip and swirl about our "irons" before taking them out of the tank, shaking them to dry them a bit, and putting them away safely until the next meal. Mugs got broken or were "'alf'inched" so many of us used our own ones which varied in appearance. When I was at Boarding School at Ambleside in the Lake District it was the occasion of the Coronation of King George VI and Queen Elizabeth on the 12th May, 1937 and we were all given a souvenir mug to mark the occasion, and I used this special mug until I went out with Tom one night, but that is a story for later on.

A NAAFI van did call at the back of Morton Hall, but I think it probably went to the Camp at R.A.F. Swinderby first for it was usually late by the time it reached us. In the Autumn I can well recall kicking through the golden leaves of a sweet chestnut tree looking for a nut to nibble whilst I waited for the van to arrive and the chance to fill our mugs and purchase either a jam doughnut, rock cake or, if lucky, a "cream" bun. These three items were the sole choice as I remember. Beryl only remembers rock cakes, biscuits or fruit cake. She was then working for the Group Legal Officer, a Canadian, and she took him back tea and cake and in return he paid for her "elevenses".

Because of its relatively small size and consequent lack of facilities there was very little social life at Group. There was no cinema, only occasional dances were held when perhaps aircrew attending a Heavy Conversion Training Course at R.A.F. Swinderby might be invited to attend.

As Group H.Q. was situated in the park-like grounds of Morton Hall the distances between buildings was relatively small. At R.A.F. stations which had several hangars and large numbers of buildings for the various trades involved the personnel were often issued with sturdy R.A.F. bicycles to save time going from place to place. These bikes all had hand painted white numbers on the rear mudguard for identification purposes. Needless to say, one had to "sign for it" when it was issued and return it in a proper condition when "getting cleared" on being posted elsewhere.

Fortunately I did not have the responsibility of caring for this additional piece of R.A.F. property as when I was posted I took my faithful Raleigh bicycle with me by putting it on the train. As we were now billeted in the grounds of Morton Hall I rarely used it except to visit Bridget a couple of miles away although Beryl and I biked over to a Sgt's Mess Dance at R.A.F. Swinderby and Tom and I once went out together on a memorable bike ride.

Morton Hall was situated eight miles south west of Lincoln down a lane roughly a mile and a half from the A46 – the old Roman Fosse Way which runs from Lincoln to Cirencester passing through Newark where it crosses the river Trent on its way to Leicester. On the opposite side of the A46 lay the airfield for R.A.F. Swinderby which was where aircrew who had previously only flown in twin-engined aircraft picked up the final two members of their crew – the flight engineer and another gunner – who were now needed in the heavier four engined Lancaster and Stirling bombers that were being used as replacements for the less powerful Wellingtons and Hampdens which were being flown when I was at R.A.F. Cottesmore in 1941. Where our lane from Morton Hall joined the A46 was sited the Half Way public house. I presume it was equidistant

equidistant between Lincoln and Newark and this was my best place for picking up a lift to take me into Lincoln when I was off duty.

I usually did quite a lot of travelling by "thumbing a lift" in those days when buses were few and far between and the railway did not happen to go in the direction I wished to travel. These days it would be foolhardy to accept a lift from anyone who stopped to pick one up, as stories in newspapers and on television will verify, as horrible cases of rape and murder have occurred. In those days cars were a relative luxury not afforded by the majority, also there was very strict petrol rationing; one felt perfectly safe to accept a lift with anyone who was kind enough to stop and who had room to spare. The one danger I remember was if there were already two men in a small lorry, and the only space for you to sit was on the engine cover between them; it could become <u>very</u> hot indeed!

When waiting by the roadside for a lift it was very welcome to hear the distinctive sound of Army or R.A.F. tyres approaching in the distance, as one knew for sure that a "lift" was arriving. I always found it enjoyable to meet so many different people from all walks of life. Nevertheless I did get a surprise one day when "hitching" from Grantham to Leadenham to see my half-sister. A huge R.A.F. car, complete with pennant, pulled up for me and for the next few miles I was sitting on the back seat with a VERY high ranking uniformed R.A.F. officer whose cap peak was smothered with "scrambled egg" or, should I say, gold braid. We had a pleasant conversation for a few miles until his car turned left through a gateway towards a large private house a couple of fields away, and I left my distinguished companion to continue my journey in less exalted fashion. I have since been told that meetings took place about the invasion plans for Europe a few miles away at Fulbeck Hall. This very senior R.A.F. officer was no doubt involved in these discussions.

I am sure you will realise that "thumbing a lift" was a daylight operation, as after the hours of darkness everything was "blacked-out" and vehicles were hardly permitted any lights at all. We were free to leave Morton Hall when our duties for the day were completed but had to book back into Camp at the Guard Room by 22.30 hours unless we had a Late Night Pass. A maximum of two per week were permitted when, Cinderella-like, we had to "book in" not later than a minute before the witching-hour of midnight, namely 23.59 hours.

A day off was usually given once a week and a 48 hour Pass once a month, which was actually somewhat longer than the 48 hrs. Technically speaking your Pass would begin, for example, after duty on Friday afternoon, ending 23.59 hrs on Sunday. However, if you had a good boss, and you could get your urgent work done in time, he would give you a "Chit" to hand in at the Guard Room so that you could "book out" on your "48" about 1 p.m. For me it was then necessary to walk well over a mile to the A.46 to the Half Way House Inn and try to pick up a lift from there.

I used to use the local bus service into Lincoln for the evening which, I think, used to park in Unity Square. The only snag about this was that it was not permitted to use it solely for the return journey back to Morton Hall from Lincoln. To return to the Hall after a "48" meant hitching back from Lincoln to the Half Way House Inn and then walking back from there for over a mile on a lonely country lane which was mostly bordered by woodland. This was O.K. when it was daylight but I hated having to do this alone on nights in winter when it was too dark to see where you were putting your feet and it was necessary to look skywards constantly to see the slightly lighter night sky between the darkness of the tree tops in order to work out where the road was. I never felt 100% sure that the noises I heard (or imagined) were just the branches of the trees clashing together in the winter wind or whether there really was a German parachutist waiting to ambush me in the darkness. I have read that in the Middle Ages the Fosse Way between Lincoln and Newark was notorious for ambushes and that there were many woodland gangs such as that of "Black Jack". Centuries later, perhaps I felt their presence lingered on.

Every three months one was entitled to seven days Leave "if the exigencies of the Service permitted". Somewhat belatedly, I have today looked up the meaning of the word. "Exigency – requiring immediate attention or remedy; urgent". Happily I was not in a trade where "exigencies" were likely to occur, so I always got my leave or time off as planned. One could claim a Railway Warrant to more or less anywhere in the U.K; we were fortunate in having a very useful railway service before Mr Beeching got busy with his axe and it seemed easy and relatively cheap to travel by train. I used it regularly when at R.A.F. Coningsby for evenings out in Lincoln whenever I was off duty.

Swinderby Railway Station was half a mile from Morton Hall but I do not remember why I used it so little. Perhaps few trains stopped there as it was such a small village or I found it cheaper to walk to the A.46 and get a lift from there. It was quite a financial balancing act not to be broke by the fortnightly Pay Parade. It was a rare treat for Ken or Tom to take me out for dinner at the Grand Hotel or Albion (now called

The Barbican) in Lincoln, as they were as near broke as I was – I believe dinner cost 5/-[1] which was the maximum permitted price for a meal. Nevertheless, I was always extremely grateful that I did not have to exist on the very meagre rations doled out to the civilian population.

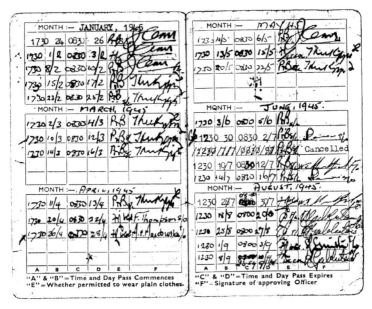

Form 295A Showing Days Off Duty in 1945/6. From H.Q. 5 Group

When Jimmy and Tom were doing their final crew training at the H.C.U. at Swinderby, I would sometimes meet one or other of them to have a day off in Nottingham together, feeling a need for a change of scene from our regular haunts in Lincoln.

----

[1] 25p

This would mean an early start in order to have breakfast, book out of Camp at the Guard Room on a Day Pass and get to the Railway Station at Swinderby in good time. Even in wartime we enjoyed looking round the shops of such a large town as Nottingham or Leicester. By noon we were searching to find a good place to eat, as my boy friends said I used to become very irritable when hungry!

After lunch we would choose a promising film to go and see, and spend a comfortable afternoon in its friendly gloom holding hands or, if we managed to get a double seat in the back row at a certain Nottingham cinema, a little snog if we were lucky!

Then something to eat at a canteen or cafe afterwards before catching the train back to Swinderby and so to our separate Camps. These journeys were relatively free of tension as operational flying for my companion was yet to come and, barring flying accidents, we should soon meet again for our evenings out together in Lincoln.

This is a copy of a combined Leave Pass and Railway Warrant issued to me to go home on compassionate Leave on 6th March 1944. Unused as it was quicker for me to hitch hike to Lincoln and then take a bus to Saxilby.

I don't know why I had this pass for a day off from noon to noon the next day – most unusual! Note number 5 of 'Instructions to Holder' – if you are in want of funds you must be ten miles or over from destination for financial help. If less – walk!

On the page 24 is a Railway Warrant issued to me on 12th October, 1945 in order to see a Medical Specialist at Nottingham Hospital. At the time I was Clerk to the Group Defence Officers at R.A.F. Morton Hall.

ROYAL AIR FORCE. R.A.F. Form 295.
(In pads of 100).

Monthly*
Temporary* }PASS* } LEAVE* }FORM

OFFICE STAMP.

CROWN COPYRIGHT RESERVED.

Station...... R.A.F. Base Station, Coningsby.

Official No. 426567 ....(Rank) Lacw (Name) Pickering, S.

has permission to be absent from his quarters, from...... 1200 ......hrs. on

6.3.44 .....to 1200 ......hrs. on 7.3.44 194

for the purpose of proceeding on ~~train~~ *pass* to Lincoln ....(Nearest Town)†

(Date)..............................

for Commanding Officer.

† If crossing Irish Sea or Eire frontier passes to R.A.F. Stations are to be
surrendered for leave period.

* Strike out word or words inapplicable.

P.T.O.

Leave/Pass Form, front and rear.

INSTRUCTIONS TO THE HOLDER.

1. Leave will expire by the time stated overleaf unless you are in possession of a sleeping-out pass entitling you to return at another time.

2. Passes will state whether monthly, for a limited period, for one occasion only, or for sleeping out.

3. This form is not valid unless bearing the stamp of the office of origin, and the signature of an officer. When on leave or pass you must carry this form with you, and must produce it on demand by Air Force, Military or Civil Police on duty.

4. When on leave, you must notify your C.O. at once of any change of your address while on leave or pass, and must be prepared at all times to rejoin on the slightest notice if ordered to do so.

5. If you are in want of funds to enable you to return at end of leave, you should apply to your C.O. for a railway warrant on repayment. If you do not receive it in time to enable you to reach your unit before expiry of leave, you should, provided that your journey exceeds 10 miles, and that there is no Air Force Unit or Air Force Recruiting Office within easy reach, report to the nearest Police Station, produce this form and ask for a warrant. The Civil Police will not issue a warrant for a journey of less than 10 miles.

6. If in London without means of reaching your destination, you should report to Air Ministry Unit or a R.T.O.

SICKNESS ON LEAVE.

The rules for getting medical attention whilst on leave are contained in your Pay Book.

Wt. 36570/2272 70m 11rs 3/42 D.P.W. 51-4176

K 777025

CHARGES PAYABLE BY
THE
UNDER SECRETARY OF STATE
AIR MINISTRY (F.3(c)),
LONDON, W.C.2.

This Warrant becomes void after 30 days from date of issue.

Date 12 — 10 — 194 5

To the *Concerned* RAILWAY COMPANY.

Please issue without charge to the bearer, ticket(s) as shown below :—

Name, Service Number and Rank of Passenger (or person in charge of party) *CPL. PICKERING*

State whether R.A.F., R.A.F. Reserve, A.A.F. or R.A.F.V.R. *WAAF*

Duty on which proceeding *medical appointment*

Authority for journey *HQ 5 GROUP*
(No. of Route or other authority.)
(Quote Air Ministry authority where known.)

Overseas Command†
(and station or country).

This Warrant is chargeable against *Air Force Funds*

This space must NOT be left blank. Insert "Air Force Funds" or name of person, department, &c.

FROM *SWINDERBY* TO *NOTTINGHAM*	‡Single. Return

At authorised Military fares	Number of Passengers (in words)		
	1st Class	2nd Class	3rd Class
ADULTS			
Children over 3 and under 14 years of age : Half Fares	ONE		ONE

Signature of Issuing Officer *J. Cann.*

Departmental or other Rank *1/L*

Unit *HQ (UNIT) 5 GROUP*

To be filled in by Railway Company.	Class			Amount payable		
	1st	2nd	3rd	£	s.	d.
Route via						
Authorised Military Fares						
Nos. of tickets issued						
Issued by .... Date						
				£	s.	d.
CHARGE FOR EXCESS ACCOMPANIED BAGGAGE SHEWN ON BACK HEREOF						

GOVERNMENT RAILWAY PASSENGER WARRANT.

This Warrant is not transferable. It must be presented at the Booking Office at the Station where the holder or party is authorised to commence the journey, when a Railway Ticket or Tickets will be issued in exchange.

Tickets must in every case be issued via the recognised direct and cheapest route.

Any alteration in this warrant must be initialled by a responsible officer.

*If not travelling individually, full particulars to be given on reverse of officers, airmen and their families (including ages of children).

†Insert particulars when a journey is to or from a port of embarkation or disembarkation, also when families proceed to or from a selected place of residence consequent upon overseas posting of personnel (give overseas command to which, or from which, posted).

‡ Strike out word inapplicable.

Railway Warrant-12th Oct 1945.

3. *Promotion!*

After a few months my bosses suggested that I should go on an N.C.O's Course. If I passed the exams, this would result in a little more pay and a few privileges. Not surprisingly I believe the Colonel and the S/Ldr were somewhat taken aback when I turned down their kind offer of recommending me for such a Course. I explained that I was very happy as I was working for them. If I became a Corporal I should be moved to other duties elsewhere in order to be in charge of people, as there was no point in the R.A.F. giving me a pay rise and extra privileges unless additional responsibilities were given to me in return. I did not want to risk being moved to an Orderly Room, or somewhere similar, where I believed I should have to give orders and, in turn, be under the control of senior N.C.Os.

The Colonel and the S/Ldr made no comment at the time, but they must have pulled a lot of strings on my behalf, for it was not long before I was told that if I was successful and did gain my "tapes" on the Course, I would not be moved elsewhere but I could still come back and work for them as before. This was amazing news, as the vacancy I occupied as their clerk certainly would not have entitled them to have a WAAF N.C.O. working for them. This meant that by going on the N.C.O's Course I would have everything to gain and nothing to lose. Most unusual! I also liked the idea of going back to R.A.F. Coningsby on an N.C.O's Course as I had been posted from there to Group H.Q. as "a Bolshie" only a few

25

months previously. Naturally enough I hoped that news of my improved status would filter through to Station Sick Quarters. It probably never did and I did not go over to see anyone there whilst I was on the Course.

In my old notebook (written in pencil because "Biros" had not been invented and fountain pens tended to run out of ink or cause blots) which I used on the Course I see that the first day was the 29th August and that I was in Hut 18. At the back of the book are autographs of sixteen other Waffs who were on the Course and the names of the Stations from which they had been sent. The following sets out the subjects that were covered in a WAAF N.C.O's Course over fifty years ago. I wonder what the Syllabus includes these days?

H.Q. 5 GROUP (BOMBER COMMAND) R.A.F. MORTON HALL

Marks:	40%	Drill
	40%	Written exam (2)
	10%	oral exam
	10%	general conduct and appearance.
We are here because:		
		Navy and Army N.C.Os – comparison.
		R.A.F. Junior Service; rapid expansion.
		WAAFs were spoon fed at first. Admin. Staff cut (A.209/43) – all N.C.Os must have powers of leadership.
DRILL:		Commands on <u>RIGHT</u> foot. Halt. Change step. Saluting to front on march. Forward from marking time. Turning at the Halt - By numbers – Calling out the time - Judging time. Changing step on the march. Marking time. Turning about.
SALUTING:		To the front (3 down) Right or left (6 down) On march (Flight in open order)
R.A.F. Organisation		- Members of the Air Council - Air Ministry Departments - Commands

	- WAAF History such as A.M.O. A.466/11 - WAAF made (20.6.41) Members of the Armed Forces of the Crown.
FIRE:	On discovering a fire. Dangers of fire being caused.
STATION ORGANISATION:	S.H.Q. Station Commander. Stn. Adjutant - no establishment for Asst/Adjt now but one is usually scrounged. Central Registry. P.O.Rs – Security. Gas - types and effects. Difference between Gas Cleansing Centre and Personal Cleansing Point. The R.A.F. Catering Organisation - By-products. Scale of Rations - Daily Ration entitlement.
WAAF ADMIN	- which Forms were used and for what purpose. Leave – Privilege, Compassionate, Embarkation, Special, Sick, Pending invaliding from Service
FIRE EXTINGUISHERS	of all types were discussed – when to use etc.
RECLASSIFICATION	Remustering – Remustering for inefficiency.
PAY AND ALLOWANCES	
EQUIPMENT SCALE	Issues, Return & Receipt, Repayment
DISCIPLINE:	Disobedience; Insubordination; Assistance or Connivance in Desertion; Absence Without Leave. Scandalous conduct of an Officer. Airwomen only - deficiency in or injury to equipment. Charges. Summary punishments. Minor punishments. Arrest and Custody. Responsibility of Duty N.C.O.

I find it interesting that we had the same ration entitlement as the men for tea, sugar, marg, salmon, herrings, sardines and butter but slightly less bread, flour, beef (boneless), cheese, bacon and preserves. For example 1 1/7th oz daily jam for the R.A.F. but 1 9/14ths oz for WAAF. Bacon - R.A.F. 1 2/7th oz per day; 1 1/7th oz per day for WAAF. Not that I can ever remember seeing salmon or herring. If they had been available – that is the amount we should have been allowed!

When serving my two happy years at R.A.F. Cottesmore I got myself excused from WAAF Morning Parade by S/Ldr Johnson in order to prepare his morning post before he came on duty. At R.A.F. Coningsby I went straight to Station Sick Quarters for breakfast and did not leave the building until the end of the day. So on both these Stations the only parades attended were Pay Parades and, at R.A.F. Cottesmore, an occasional Funeral Parade.

Therefore, the fact that on this N.C.O's Course I had to drill a squad filled me with apprehension. I had not done any drilling myself since those icy January days in Harrogate in 1941 when I first volunteered for the WAAF and we used to be marched and drilled amongst the frozen flower beds of that Spa town. As a result I was not used to hearing Drill commands, let alone executing them myself or getting a Squad under my command to do so. My worst terror occurred when marching my Squad away from me across the vast emptiness of the Parade Ground and worrying whether I should be able to give the command "About Turn" on the correct foot, for if I hesitated for too long, either the girls would not be able to hear me, or they would disappear into the distance beyond recall!

Happily all went well and I studied so hard that I found no difficulty with the written papers. In order to redeem my tarnished reputation I put everything into doing as well as I could on this Course. I now, shamefacedly admit that, when discussing a written paper with the WAAF Officer afterwards, seriously querying why I had only been given 97% on one paper when all my answers were correct! Where had I lost that 3%? I do remember she appeared nonplussed by my question – to ease the situation I think I suggested it must have been because my handwriting was so poor or something like that!

I think our Course was No. 17 or 18 and it transpired that I obtained the highest mark ever recorded on the N.C.O's Course so a special letter of commendation was sent from R.A.F. Coningsby to Group about my unexpected achievement. I do not remember being told of the results officially but I know the Colonel and S/Ldr were very pleased for me and I was most grateful to them and so thankful that I could continue working for my two super officers as before my promotion. As a Leading Aircraftwoman (similar rank to Lance Corporal) I was being paid 4/4d. per day. From 3rd September, 1944 it was increased to the princely sum of 5/-[1] per day as I then became a corporal.

It was the usual practice for our huts to contain either day or shift workers, as otherwise the "comings and goings" of shift workers inevitably caused sleep disturbance for day workers. Before I went on the N.C.O's course I slept in a hut of clerks and the Corporal in charge of our hut had her own little room partitioned off at the end of it.

After the N.C.O.s course the "powers that be" must have thought that they were now the "proud possessors" of a newly discovered "star" who had shone quite brilliantly on the Course. They had promised not to move her away from her previous job, so what was the best way to utilise this talent?

I have mentioned before that on weekly hut inspections some huts came in for a great deal of criticism by the WAAF Inspecting Officer. Ergo, put this ex "Bolshie" WAAF suddenly turned "brilliant" N.C.O. in charge of the dirtiest and scruffi-

----

[1] 25p per day

est hut which was full of shift workers. This hut had never had an N.C.O. in charge of it before and there was not even a partitioned space at one end for an N.C.O. to have any privacy. Her every move (literally) was in full view of all other inmates. I was supposed to take control of them and bring them up to standard in keeping the hut in good order. Phew!

There was no way out for me. It was no good my saying "I can't do it" – my good results on the Course were only achieved because I was so angry at the way I had been treated when I was at S.S.Q. at Coningsby. They were just freakish marks. Please don't throw this poor little Christian Corporal into that hut full of lionesses! Our feelings were mutual. I did not want to move into their hut. They did not want me in with them

The girls would have known that I had just been made up to the rank of Corporal, as such items were published in D.R.O's.[1] I was not even of the same trade as they were. We had nothing in common. When I lay in bed at night trying to get to sleep, and listened to the conversation of girls coming off or going on duty, I often had difficulty in understanding all that they said. I had never before been aware that there were so many, usually quite short words, that began with the letter "b…!". Conversing in a perfectly normal sort of manner, it seemed that about every fourth or fifth word began with "b". It was fascinating listening to them in a horrible sort of way.

My problems started before I went off to breakfast and then straight on to the office, as I was responsible for seeing that the hut was left neat and tidy and the floor space rea-

---

[1] Daily Routine Orders

sonably clean each day. There always seemed to be a great deal of activity in the hut with some of the girls either coming in off duty, preparing to go on duty or sleeping. When I commented that a particular bed-space needed cleaning up, there always seemed to be someone able to give me a reason why it had not been done and why the owner of the bed-space could not do it at that time. I had no way of knowing if the excuses I was given were genuine. I only knew that they were waiting to see if they could rile me so much that I would put someone on a Charge. However, I felt that if I gave them the slightest reason to dislike me personally, they would have made my life in the hut intolerable.

Even after Monday Camp Night all the bed spaces were still not polished ready for Tuesday morning inspection. I did them myself. Gradually the attitude of the girls towards me changed as they found that I was not throwing my weight around as a newly made-up Corporal but using it instead on the heavy "bumper" or floor polisher on the unpolished bed spaces! The comments of the WAAF Inspecting Officer steadily improved until it was usual for our Hut to be in the top three – or even top – after Tuesday hut inspection. It was wonderful when I even got to the stage when the only bed space I cleaned was my own. My Hut of very rough diamonds shone in all their glory at last. Incredible.

Apart from being in charge of the hut, my only other duty, which did not come round very often, was that of Duty Clerk at night in the Hall. After all the office staff had finished for the day I went on duty in a little office on the ground floor. Throughout the evening and night I was responsible for getting any urgent late post listed and prepared for the appropriate Despatch Riders who rode up on their motorbikes to collect this after signing for it with their name and time of collection. I think one came about midnight and the other somewhat later. I then checked that everything was safely locked up and dozed on the camp bed left in the office for that purpose. Beryl also did this night duty and remembers that one despatch rider came from H.Q. 1 Group at Bawtry with films/photos of the night's raids. They were in metal containers and arrived about 5 a.m. or in the early hours depending on what time targets were bombed. She says she nearly always looked at a few before delivering them to the appropriate Departments.

4. *Ken*

According to one of Ken's letters we met on 19th February, 1944. Strangely enough I can still remember the meeting. It was in an upstairs Dance Hall not far from the Stonebow in Lincoln – I believe it is now a Snooker Hall. Having had a deep friendship with another Australian I immediately noticed the distinctive dark blue uniform of an Aussie aircrew member on the dance floor. He was tall, dark, good looking and a superb dancer. I wanted above all else for this Aussie to be my dancing partner but with all those girls wearing civvies – pretty frocks and long flowing hair – what chance had I of getting my wish!

Although I had been in the WAAF for three years I was still, underneath it all, greatly lacking in self confidence. Unfortunately, in order to try to mask this fact, I was often accused of appearing rather supercilious and of being "toffee-nosed" and haughty. I sometimes smoked a cigarette on these occasions in order to appear "occupied" as it gave me something to do with my hands whilst hopefully waiting to be asked to dance.

I realised that when looking for a potential partner one's eyes tended to look to the other side of the room across the dance floor rather than close by. So, when my "quarry" left the dance floor I went to the side of the room opposite to him and tried to look quite happy and fully occupied – without a glance in his direction. Luckily my strategy worked – this gorgeous Aussie (the only one in the room) came across,

33

introduced himself and asked me for a dance. With his strong arm around me I felt in Heaven! (How youngsters can enjoy dancing these days – with bodies rarely touching – beats me!)

Ken – 14th April, 1944

I thanked my lucky stars that I had been tutored so well at the Victoria Dance Hall in Oakham by F/Sgt. "Brush" Blowers, the Link Trainer Instructor, who regularly used to cycle in from R.A.F. North Luffenham and meet me at the Dance Hall when

I took the bus in to Oakham from R.A.F. Cottesmore in the autumn of 1942.

Let me introduce Ken my new dancing partner. He was an Australian Mid Upper Gunner of 460 Royal Australian Air Force Squadron who flew Lancaster bombers. Ken's home was near the River Murray in Victoria, Australia where he lived at home with his parents and worked on a fruit farm grading fruit before it went into the packing sheds.

Ken and I enjoyed each other's company a great deal and used to meet in Lincoln to dance whenever possible although it was not easy for him to get into Lincoln from the top of the Lincolnshire Wolds where R.A.F. Binbrook was situated.

I took Ken home with me on 48 hour Leave Passes and he got on very well with my Father. Ken wasn't squeamish about gutting a chicken or skinning a rabbit – I think such attributes were appreciated by my Father as proving Ken was a practical and useful potential son-in-law. Nevertheless my Father was always a most inconveniently strict chaperon. Even now I can remember when my Father was working in the garden, so Ken and I went up the attic stairs to the maid's old bedroom to enjoy a good "snog"! In a very short time it seemed that my Father left his gardening and stood in the hallway calling up "What are you both doing up there? Come on down". The spoil-sport.

I could not make up my mind how I truly felt about Ken as we were able to spend so little time together. You do not really get to know someone on the dance floor, when having dinner out together at the "Grand" on the rare occasions we could afford to do so or even spending a "48" together at Saxilby. Much to my Father's disgust I arranged to go on leave with Ken and part of his crew to Edinburgh. From the following letters you will see that it was difficult to arrange our Leaves to coincide. We travelled together up to Edinburgh by train overnight and the journey seemed long and tiring. Ken's crew seemed a tough lot, talked little and I don't think we had much in common. They stayed at the Cockburn Hotel and Ken and I had separate rooms at another very good, large hotel where there was dancing every night after dinner and food rationing seemed non-existent. I remember we went window gazing down Princes Street, visited Holyrood Palace and Edinburgh Castle with plenty of stops for snacks as there was so much lovely food available.

By the end of our Leave together I knew that Ken would make a superb husband as he was honest, loyal, kind, hardworking and had all the virtues possible. But, I would not make him the wife he so richly deserved. I was very fond of Ken but I was not in love with him.

(August 1944)

My Darling,

Just a little reminder to let you know I haven't forgotten you and I love you more than ever and shall be thinking of you all day Sunday. Am so sorry I never got you a present but am sure we shall be able to decide on one when we go to Scotland.

Cheerio Darling,

Many Happy returns for the 27th August.

From,

Yours devotedly Always,

Now and Ever

Ken

S W A L K X

Binbrook
Monday, 18th September, 1944

Darling,

Was ever so glad to receive your letter today and of course I am not angry because you never wrote on Friday, would have been most annoyed if you would have wasted the time instead of seeing Les.[1] I am so glad you seen him alright. Also am quite relieved that you never exercised Giddy[2] as I know you weren't in the best of health. Perhaps that explains why you never appeared in a very good mood, I do hope you never hurt Les after coming all that way to see you darling. He really must like you Sylvia, why you bother about a twerp like me I don't know. I would most certainly like to meet Les, one of these days.

Gosh I reckon you were in a flat spin when you discovered you were at the wrong station. What would you have done had you missed it would you been able to get back early next day. If you had done that would you have been on a Charge for staying out without an S.O.P.?[3]

This Tom seems to be rather a jealous sort of a customer over Jimmy doesn't he. Why should he be, after all I don't see why you shouldn't go out with him in preference of staying home. Doesn't do any harm to go out an about with some body different.

Thanks ever so much darling for going to all that bother getting all those Hotel addresses as you did seem so terribly cheesed, but it was awfully sweet of you and I shall not forget it. I haven't any particular reason to go up to Aberdeen only to see that lass I told you about. But I just thought it would be nice if we would go up there for a day or so and then come down to E'bor or some other place and have a look around. I'm not so particular where I

----

[1] My friendship with Leslie began in January 1941 and our meeting is described in Chapter Two of my previous book.

[2] My horse

[3] Sleeping Out Pass

go darling as long as it is with you I don't mind. We could still get our Rail Warrant made out to Aberdeen and if only went to E'bor it shouldn't make any difference should it. I can tell you that our leave is definitely the 4th now and we shall be putting in for our leave next Sunday. As you say you wouldn't have any trouble to get accommodation in a YWCA but I don't want you to go there if I can avoid it. We could go up to E'bor and stay the 1st night and perhaps go to Glasgow or Aberdeen for a day and see if we could get accommodation if not come back to E'bor.

I think we could have a good look around from E'bor, a day here and a day some place else and a dance every night that's the shot. Ford & Reg are going up to E'bor I think this leave. You never know what I may be likely to do at the last minute if I were to run into one of these good oh girls at Cleethorpes or Grimsby but I shall do my best to stay clear if possible.

Went to the Camp Cinema last night with Ford, Viv & Reg. I seen this "Iris in ?Mo?" show quite a light show and I enjoyed it, pretty old I think.

Got up for parade this morning bags of bull this squadron is becoming unbearable last night they were the only one in the group that never operated to our disgust. There isn't anything on tonight either so we will be able to go into Grimsby to a show.

The trip the other night was quite O.K. seen plenty of flak but no fighters. I thought we would as it was a Jerry airfield we pranged in Germany. I guess the remaining ones are going to take a while to come.

Afraid I must get along to catch the post. Cheerio and all the best till to-morrow.

Your Pal Always.

Ken

X X X X X

My Dear Sylvia,

Was great hearing from you again today and by the way I have wrote up to the Cockburn in E'bor for accommodation from 5th til 9th do you think that shall be O.K. with you. Thought we could go over to Leadenham and catch that train I caught last time I went up. Or would you rather go on an earlier train. It is all the same to me darling. Whatever you suggest goes with me. So you are surprised at Viv going with a married woman. Why shouldn't (he) after all he is married himself why spoil us single lads chances. As you say I most certainly don't need any encouragement to go astray just wait until this here tour is over, will I have a good time. Just ask me will I. Afraid to say that Viv is going to E'bor after all his girl friend's husband got his final leave and so she has taken her 9 days now and so he is going to Tamworth and B'ham again. I think that Reg & Ford are going to E'bor but am not certain yet.

Yes Reg's face is quite O.K. again and we might be able to get the usual one a week in O.K.

It hasn't turned out such a wizard mascot after all. The boys reckon it is a jinx and call him the Wingless Wonder. It stays on the ground with the ground crew. They will not allow him to fly on ops as he hasn't given us enough confidence as since we got him & we would rather go without him. I wrote and told Beat too, so I gather she will be both disappointed & upset. So you would have been proud to provide a mascot for Murrays Mob, should have got to know you a few months sooner and maybe we could have done something about it.

Do you realise that it is just 7 months today since you had the misfortune of meeting, what a changed person I am now. I bet you have seen a big change in me. I was telling Viv about you hinting of some way to get to a warmer climate and told him my suggestion to you and then I told him what you said today. He asked me to ask you if he should buy you a new fishing line as the one you have must be worn out. I'm afraid I don't see the humour or the sense in it. So I hope you do.

So glad to hear that you never put on weight while you were on the Course[1] and 9 st 10 lbs is a most excellent weight for a big girl like you. Darling, I am proud of you. But what's this about me needing a few more lbs. I don't think I am that bad, I am just thinking of doing some daily P.E. to get into a good condition for when I go home again.

Your not telling me anything babe when you tell me I will have to get me a wife who is a good cook to look after me I also want one who loves me & and I want to love her as equally as much. I might even over look the fact of her not being such a good cook, we could always eat out until she became quite domesticated. No I am afraid you have got me wrong about a wife. I might have said they would make a good baby producer & good foot warmer but that's only a blind. I want one who would be a good companion for life, would give & take, what ever happens, so I could tease her while she is washing up <u>&</u> help her also might even think of giving her breakfast in bed occasionally, but that would be spoiling her don't you think. What about giving your opinion after all you are a girl and a future wife you should be able to give me some 1st hand information which may really help me, in the very near future. Have to hurry up and do something or I am afraid I'm going to be left on the shelf.

I presume you mean Margaret would make a good substitute for Joan, you said Joan but must have got a bit mixed. No I haven't bothered to go to Gy[2] with her yet she is at present on holiday but should be back any day.

What do you mean your tummy isn't as bad as it used to be. Its quite bad enough & I think something should be done about it if it is going to continue and give you those bad attacks. Your one of those folk who won't give in till you have to then sometimes it

----

[1] N.C.O's Course

[2] Grimsby

is too late. You say don't worry darling I shall be O.K. in time. How long, that's what I would like to know.

I only wish I could be with you to look after you when your tummy plays up. I would put you to bed and look after you personally, even call a doctor in and see what he reckons. So if anything were to happen while in E'bor, you know whats going to happen, so don't say I never warned you.

Yes it was great to get that cable from Mum & it relieved me quite a bit. I do wish dad would hurry home I shall tell you what he said in his letter when I see you next.

What gave you the hunch that we would be on our 20th Sunday night. We went at one o'clock in the morning. Actually would like to get up to pass the 25 mark before leave, but I don't think we have much chance.

There wasn't anything on last night so we all went into Gy & seen "Canterbury Tale". I thoroughly enjoyed it myself, you seen it with Les I think. Believe there is nothing on again tonight for us. I am getting fed up with this deluge. Still never mind only a fortnight to hold out before our leave again. Won't it be wizard to have you with me for 6 days. I won't want to leave you at all after that.

Did a bit of P.T. this morning, got my new Flgt/Com.[1] So we shall have to drum him the score and tell him we don't like that kind of business.

Afraid I must away as it is after 2 p.m. & I should be up the Flight to sign on & the mail closes 2.30. – I mustn't miss it.

Cheerio and all the best,

Yours,

Ken

X X X X X ?

---

[1] Flight Commander

Binbrook
20th September 1944

Dear Sylvia,

I was ever so glad to get your letter today and will endeavour to write you a short reply as we are anticipating a training flip and are likely to be off any time, so I don't know for how long I shall be able to carry on with this.

The Col[1] is getting rather considerate allowing you to write letters in his time, don't you think. Yes, I will be quite glad to get back to Aussie to go to a few dances again. Its not that the bands or the floors are any better, but I do think this is because I know most of the folk who go to them all, and I think that that goes a long way when you can go to a hall and say hullo to almost everyone. Have been to quite a few dances since I have been in this country but the friendly atmosphere is not the same in my opinion. But I must say that the average girl over here are better dancers than those over home. Maybe I am getting homesick after all, sick of being away from my mother.

So you and Tom have been disagreeing again, he is getting nearly as bad as me at having a bust up with you, don't you think. Do hope you are able to smooth things over and be good friends again, but I don't see why you should have to sacrifice a boy friend or so just because of him, still after all that is your affair and who am I to say or interfere with your ideas. I think you are making yourself miserably unhappy over nothing at all, don't worry over somebody who dislikes you going out with other fellows, its not reasonable I ask you. I'm afraid you must be in love with him after all. Still you can't say I never put any opposition for him and I am disappointed that I lost to a better man, but am I down hearted, Just ask me. Have you told Tom you are going to Scotland with me. Gosh if you have I think I will refuse to go with

---

[1] Colonel – my boss

you as Tom may get really desperate and "moider me". Still I would be willing to take the chance if your still game enough.

If you find it too much of a bind to write every day, don't hesitate to cut them down as I don't want you to write if you don't feel like it.

You have the right idea about allowing other people to decide on things and letting them take the blame, that is if you can get the mug to take it for you, I have always been the mug though, so it is no new role for me.

I shall be sure to let you know if the accommodation is O.K. Should get a reply early in the next week. You could get your rail warrant still to Aberdeen and if we only go to Edin'boro, no harm done, you can always say you are getting the next train or some such excuse, knowing your ability you should be able to stall off an S.P.[1] without flickering an eye lid.

Hope you were able to have that day off with Tom. I nearly rang you at ¼ to 4 yesterday and came over to Lincoln myself. Just as well I did change my mind as I guess you had a date Tom intended to come back this morning as there wasn't anything doing. We all went to the Camp show instead Golden Horn. Would have been too much of a rush for me to get over there, and I guess you were happy as you would no doubt have seen Tom if he was going on leave.

What arrangements have you decided on about boy friends. Don't tell me I am still on your list, yes but at the bottom I bet.

Cheerio Pal, I can still fall for you in a big way too. If you really believe me.

Yours,

Ken

X X X X X

---

[1] Service Police

Spilsby
20th September 1944

Hullo My Darling,

You will have to excuse the paper as I couldn't buy a pad at this dump and Fred was so generous and came to my rescue with this log so I could write you a few lines darling.

As I told you yesterday we were expecting to go on a training flip. This we done and had the misfortune to be diverted to Spilsby where I am at present. If you remember we were diverted here once before on our 3rd op. It is not a bad little dump but it is 5 Group and of course I belong to the gen[1] Group. Don't take it so hard darling, as after all the truth hurts sometimes.

I did intend to write you a letter tonight when we got back, as I usually have to rush them if I write them the same day and as I have nothing to do this is a good chance.

I have just heard there is a stand down here tonight and also a dance so I think we shall have to gate crash even though we are in flying boots, should be quite a novelty don't you think.

Just imagine this time in a fortnight I hope to be beside you darling on our way for those 6 glorious days. I am certain we will have a grand time. I suppose at this minute 5 past 8 to be correct, you are with Tom yourself as you were to have today with him, that is if you were able to patch everything up O.K. Trust you were able to but hope you never had to sacrifice any of your boy friends If so, it wasn't me. How many "ops" has Tom done now – must be in double figures by now. He looks like beating us at the rate we are progressing. I think we shall be here for a long time yet. We don't mind as there is a big possibility of us flying Queenie back to Aussie but we are still on the Squadron at the end of next month. Looks like as if I shall see Xmas at home yet Gosh that shall be hard to take.

---

[1] Ken was in 460 R.A.A.F. Squadron of No. 1 Group

I think I shall sign off and go to the dance and see what I can pick up. Might be able to pick up a WAAF as beautiful as yourself, but I doubt if I could find a better pal than you anywhere and wouldn't need to unless you decided to give me the go by. Wonder if you will.

Thursday 21st September. 9 o'clock. Hullo Darling. Here I am once again to annoy you with a few more lines. Do hope you are able to read this O.K. as I know it is quite a mess. Yes I went to the dance and I wish to relieve your mind by telling you are still No. 1 girl friend for me. Went to the dance but that is all. I left the place as fast as I went in. The WAAFs were a terrible lot and the airmen outnumbered them 4 to 1, so I ask you what sort of a chance do you think I would have had. It takes me all my time to land one when the situation is in reverse.

So I went back and turned in and dreamt about our leave in a fortnight. Gosh won't it be great to think that in a fortnight we shall be in E'boro together. Do hope that nothing happens to interfere with our arrangements. We will be definite for starting our leave on 4th now. What do you intend to do, are you going to get from the 3rd to 12th or are you going to have the 4th till 13th. Will we go over to Leadenham on the afternoon or would you rather catch one on the Thursday. I think it would be better if we could get that night train then we should be in E'boro 8 o'clock Thursday morn. Not going to York as we had expected means I shall not meet Les but perhaps I may get the chance before long again.

Where did Tom go for leave? I think I shall go down to Devon for my next leave that may be my embarkation leave. Gosh I am thrilled to think it may be that. It hardly seems possible that I may see everyone by Xmas. Gosh I bet you shall be glad to get rid of me – so will Tom to think that you are getting a few less boy friends, still I guess you will soon get some more to annoy him.

Well the news doesn't seem to be the best today so goodness knows when we shall get off from here still why worry, I guess we shall get off in due course, I don't suppose there shall be anything on.

You shall have to forgive me for the pencil and paper but it is the best I could do. Afraid I haven't got any further news for the present so will sign off til next time.

Yours Affectionately Always
Now and Ever
Ken

R.A.F. Binbrook, Lincs.
23rd Sept 1944

Dearest Sylvia,

I must 1st of all apologise for my abrupt ending to my letter yesterday, but as Ken came in and said we were flying at ¼ to 2 and it was then 12 I had to have lunch and I also wanted you to get a letter today and so I had to end it as quickly as possible. Even almost overlooked that you have got your CplW. Gosh had I not noticed that when I did and said something about it I guess you would never have forgiven me. It was only lucky that I did so as I had already addressed it to an Lacw Pickering. I wonder if she is still the same girl I knew. Something seems to tell me that she has changed, I wonder. Soon have a chance to find out as it shall not be very much longer before we go on that long awaited leave together, even though it seems as if we may have some difficulties in getting accommodation, but I am still trying and if we are not successful will go up there and hope to get in somewhere even if it were just out of E'bor. Our leave is only the usual 6 days from AD[1] on the 4th till 0900 hrs on the 11th. Hope to get away from here about lunch time and get in to Lincoln on the bus between 1 & 2 o'clock. If I can hitch hike it will be a lot faster, shall do my best. I could then come over to Saxilby and pick you up and then we could go on to E. Retford, Doncaster, York as you suggest darling you are getting to good a navigator Fred says, seems

---

[1] After Duty

to think we may dump him for you and wouldn't commit himself by making a statement. But he never said he could pick a better route. I just suggest going down to Grantham as I thought you might like to go through Leadenham and catch that train I caught last time, but I am easy. Do you think there is any chance of seeing Les if we go to York I would like to meet him.

Yes, it is bad luck that the Wingless Wonder is such a gremlin but I don't think he is that bad myself, its just that the boys are getting a little superstitious after having gone so far, but of course I have not taken him if they are all against him as I guess they would never forgive me if anything was to happen.

Viv does not seem to mind not going to E'bor as he will be just as at home in B'ham and is going down there, - it must be rather awkward when the husband comes home, don't forget to tell me when yours is likely to be around. Yes, it was Viv, Gordon and Reg you met that night in the Toc H. Since when you have apparently deteriorated in his ideas, don't know why though, probably it was because I told him we were in bed together. Do you think I would be game I would never hear the end of it from the crew. I told him exactly what you suggested to me did I offer ideas of getting to a warmer climate and you said you could volunteer for service in India. I said I thought that a good scheme and I told Viv what you had said and told him my reply. His answer was It's not exactly the answer she expected you dope. She is asking you to marry her what more could you want.

Then he suggested that it was time you were given a new fishing rod and offered to present you with one. He can only offer a rod however and one new line that's himself of course but I told him he would have to be very careful as at present you have a few jealous boy friends who were rather desperate at the moment and wouldn't stop at anything less than murder just now. So will wait until things blow over a little bit.

Have just received yesterday's letter and I was thinking you had the day off and intended to ring you to-day so I guess that is out until to-morrow even then I will not ring as you never replied to my question on what was your ext. no. So I can't very well ring you until you oblige me with that, I am disappointed with you, so you don't want me to ring you, alright then I won't.

See you went to the Sgts' Mess Dance at Swinderby, showing off those stripes that's all I can say. Had quite a good time. Alright tell me and put me out of my misery you have another boy friend well what of it. Do you ever think that you will ever get sick of many and be contented to settle down with one, because I am beginning to be doubtful. Gosh, how will Tom take it don't tell me I can guess, will he explode like dynamite, but for all I know it may have been him as he is on leave. Still why should I worry and lose sleep I gave that up long ago since meeting you. Its women like you who drive men crazy that is if they are silly enough to be allowed to be driven that way.

No there shall be no need to go to Grantham and we can catch a train at York O.K. that one I caught goes through there at 2.30 a.m. or thereabouts, shall be an awful wait around, still I won't mind, I won't be scared with you to look after me darling. I do wish we could get at least 4 or 5 ops in before then but I doubt if we shall get 2 more in at the rate we are going. After all the trouble we went to they scrubbed our trip yesterday, but Ken, Gordon, Fred and Viv took a crew over to Spilsby to pick up their kite that had been left there for repairs. Was no need for gunners or B/A[1] I would have went had they been staying a while, but I could never have seen Alf so never bothered, stayed back and wrote some more mail.

Well I think I have exhausted all my news for the present and shall have to sign off again for the present. So Cheerio and all the best. Am longing to see you again.

As Fond as Ever
Yours Ken
X X X X X ?

---

[1] Bomb Aimer

11 P.D.R.C. BRIGHTON
Sussex
29.Oct (1944)

Dear Sylvia,

This shall come as quite a surprise to you no doubt as when you were down on leave it seemed as if I would be over here some-time yet, but I am afraid that I shall not be here much longer as mother's health had deteriorated and having applied to go home am now waiting to catch the next boat. That goes on about the 9th Nov. and so I should be home for Xmas. I'm quite excited at the thought. I have sent them a cable so they shall be equally thrilled I expect.

So I will not take up any further of your time, pal. But thanks a million for everything you have done, I shall never ever forget you.

Best of luck to you and Jimmy and regards to everyone.
God Bless you,
Ken

VICTORIA,
AUSTRALIA
9th November (1944)

My Dear Sylvia,

I was ever so glad to receive your always welcomed letter yes-terday. I do hope that this finds you as well as it leaves me for the present. Full up to the teeth with excitement as to-morrow we start on the way home and so this my last few lines to wish you farewell pal.

Yes I am sure that the news of my home coming shall be a grand tonic for mother.

Yes I am very sorry to be going so soon myself, but after all one only has one mother, and I would hate anything to happen to her while I was away.

I too have appreciated your great friendship and companion-ship as you have always been grand to me. I want to thank you for those happy memories that I have got to look back on.

No sorry pal I haven't got a photo in W/O's uniform doubt if I shall get one taken now as I shall be in civvies by the time I get back home.

Ever so glad to hear that Jimmy has progressed so well, and I hope that he gets his discharge right away, and that you get yours in January, but don't go overdoing the riding for a start.

I am sure that you shall be able to handle "Red Wine" O.K., apparently most people underestimate you. My you must have had a decent sort of hunt the other day. Gosh 7½ hrs in the sad-dle, I would physically be on crutches after that time.

Well Sylvia I shall leave you here as I have a lot more letters to write, so regards to all.

The very best of Happiness to you and Jimmy. Also Merry Xmas and Happy New Year.

Your Pal Always,

God Bless,

Ken

Ken 19th August, 1944.

Ken and I never discussed where he had been on ops and I never knew how many he did before returning to his homeland. Therefore, I was pleased to receive a letter from The Hon. MacKenzie Wright OAM from Australia dated 23rd February, 2003. In it he stated: "Ken did thirty-one ops – most over Germany. He did seven ops in ten days."

5. *Tom and the Bike Ride*

Beryl and I first met Tom in June 1944 when he and some of his friends cycled over from R.A.F. Swinderby to a little dance which was being held in our NAAFI at Morton Hall. I know we got on very well together and spent most of the time talking about horses as I don't remember anything about Tom's prowess on the dance floor. Tom was a great fellow, always good company and full of fun and we regularly enjoyed our free time together whenever it could be arranged. Nevertheless I never felt that I knew the "real" Tom, only the side of himself that he showed to the outside world. When I quizzed him about his home and family in Australia he used to laughingly reply with another question "You know that big Department Store in London called Whiteleys?" – that was all the reply I got! Whiteley was his surname.

One day Tom and I were spending our day off together in Nottingham and, most unusually, were having tea in quite a smart hotel. We were sitting at a table for two with a waitress to serve us. A far cry from our more usual eating places such as the NAAFI Club or some Canteen. Then Tom took me completely by surprise. He asked me to marry him. This was very flattering and I said I was extremely fond of him but felt we did not know each other sufficiently well to enter into what was then considered a lifetime commitment to each other. Happily, I don't think Tom was surprised by my answer, and I don't remember the subject of marriage being raised again.

I had always been puzzled why such a wide variety of people seemed to enjoy becoming drunk. It did not happen to them just the once – which might have been put down to accidental over-drinking, but seemed to occur on a regular basis. I even understood that some WAAFs were afflicted in this way too. What was I missing that they all found so enjoyable? No one could give me a satisfactory explanation.

When a child, I have been told, that at lunch time I used to sit in my high chair at the right hand of my father at the dining table. He used to drink a bottle of Worthington Pale Dinner Ale with his meal and a little of it was poured into my silver Christening mug for me to enjoy. Whether or not I dunked my rusks in the amber liquid I cannot recall. When visiting relatives expressed surprise at seeing me so engaged at such a tender age, I am told that my father explained matters by saying that the barley or malt – or something – was good for me.

After coming home from Church on Sunday morning it was usual to have a piece of Madeira cake and a glass of wine – or it may have been a glass of Madeira and a piece of cake – I am not taking any bets now as to which it was. Later on it was normal to have wine with meals on special occasions.

In fact I was put off brandy and whisky for life because when I had toothache, and was awaiting emergency treatment from our dentist in Lincoln, a little swab of cotton wool was soaked in either of the above spirits and I was told to put it on the aching tooth and bite on it, and it was quite effective in giving temporary pain relief. Even now the smell of brandy or whisky revolts me, as my memory still associates the smell with childhood toothache and pain.

So you will see that I was no stranger to those liquids which were, in those days, forbidden pleasures until near adulthood had been reached. I wondered if these girls wished to drink so unwisely because all alcoholic drinks had been forbidden to them when they were young, and it was now a chance to find out for themselves if previously forbidden fruit did, indeed, taste sweeter. There was only one solution. I must try out this new experience for myself.

I knew that my drinking companion on this spree must be someone whom I could trust implicitly. Also, that wherever this binge took place it should not be where anyone might see me who would recognise me, as I did not want news of this foolishness to be spread around. Yes, you have guessed – Tom was to be my companion, and said he would look after me.

I realised that Tom would shortly be posted with his newly completed crew from Swinderby to a squadron somewhere to start operational flying. I wasn't going to risk making a fool of myself in Lincoln with the problem of getting back to Morton Hall afterwards, so it had to be done while Tom and I were within biking distance of each other.

I had still got my old Raleigh bicycle with me and we arranged that Tom would borrow a bike and ride over from R.A.F. Swinderby and meet me in the lane outside Morton Hall at a certain time one evening. Unfortunately on that particular day I was exceptionally busy in the office and worked unusually late. I was even too late to get a meal in the Mess and only had time to freshen up, book out at the Guard Room and cycle up the lane to meet Tom at the agreed time.

We did not have a map and, as the signposts had been removed to puzzle the enemy if we were invaded, I have no idea where we went. It was a lovely sunny evening and we just gently rode our bikes until we came to a pub at the edge of a village, propped up our bikes outside and went in. Having had nothing to eat since my mid-day meal I know I was very hungry and hoped we could get some sandwiches but I don't remember whether or not there were any to be had. I rather think not. I probably had some cider, as I am very fond of that. I can't remember what else I had. I think I may have been feeling gloomy as Tom told me he would probably be posted to an operational squadron the following week. This meant he might be posted too far away from Morton Hall for us to meet even when we could get our free time to coincide, or perhaps the Fates might decree that we would never meet again. I don't think we stayed in the Pub very long as I believe the atmosphere in it soon became rather smoky, which I disliked as it made my eyes smart.

The sun was sinking as we slowly cycled together along the deserted lanes back to Morton Hall. In due course I told Tom that we must stop as I wanted "to spend a penny". At the side of the lane was a convenient gate leading into a cornfield, whose crop had nearly all been led away.

Even now I can vividly remember climbing up this gate and gripping the top rail with all my might as I swung my leg over it. I was aware of the strong pull of gravity far, far greater than I had ever felt it before. I fell to the ground with a dull thud.

The sky was dark and I do not know how much time elapsed until I became aware that the moon was shining and Tom was repeatedly saying "Pull yourself together. Come on, come on, we must get back to Camp". Feeling somewhat fuddled I managed to get back on to the lane and mount my bike. Tom's voice called out sternly "Look what you are doing – follow the rear light on my bike and keep on a straight line on the lane". I replied irritably "I AM doing". My actions belied my words as by then I was cycling bumpity-bump on the grass verge once more before managing to find the smooth surface of the lane and follow Tom's, to me, dimly lit rear light.

I imagine my erratic steering went on for most of the way back to the gates of Morton Hall where we parted, and I went on up the driveway to the Guard Room to book in.

When you book out of Camp you sign the book with the time you are booking-out, the last three digits of your number, your rank and name. When you return you put in the appropriate column the time of your return, and sign it. Simple. Or so it had been on all previous occasions.

There was a huge clock on the wall of the Guard Room, similar to those which used to be found on school classroom walls. I looked at the clock to check on the time to put in the Booking-In Book. What worried me was that the clock hands would not stay still long enough for me to read the time. Both hands seemed to be in a "V" shape on the face of the clock, and swung regularly from left to right and back again, as if it was a "V" shaped pendulum. How could I write down the time if the wretched clock hands would not stay still long enough for me to read them? Before we parted Tom had warned me not to talk to anyone on my way back to the hut. Anyway, I had enough sense not to ask the Duty N.C.O. in the Guard Room to tell me what time it was, as that would have given away the state that I was in. So, after a few minutes of bafflement, I left the Guard Room without saying a word and without booking in, and so to bed.

The hut was in complete darkness, as all the black-out curtains would have been in place so the moonlight did not shine in. Eventually I located my bed and thankfully climbed into it, being momentarily puzzled by the sound of something crashing to the ground and breaking as it did so.

I slept like the proverbial log for some time but then woke up as I felt uncomfortably warm. I wondered whether or not it was nearly time to get up, or whether there was time to turn over and go to sleep again. I thought I would check on the time by looking at Roo's neat little Westclox alarm clock which he gave me to look after for him when he went on ops, saying that a number of his mates coveted it and it would "disappear" if there was a time when he did not return. I kept this little clock handily beneath my bed on my "bomb" box[1] where I could easily reach it just by stretching my arm out of bed. As I reached for the clock I was amazed to see my blue poplin shirt-sleeved arm appear from beneath the bed-clothes. It should have been covered by Air Force issue blue/white striped flannelette pyjamas!

I quickly retracted the arm into the privacy of the bed-clothes, at the same time having a quick look round at the other beds to see if anyone else was awake and had seen what I had seen.

All was well, everyone else was still fast asleep. This gave me time to assess the matter carefully. On further investigation I found that before getting into bed I had removed only my shoes, jacket and skirt. Otherwise I was still fully dressed, including my collar and tie. As it was early August, no wonder I was too warm!

The crash I had heard as I got into bed the night before was the smashing of my 1937 Coronation Mug. It, and my "irons" had been left on my bed the night before after my abortive trip to the Mess when I was too late to get anything to eat before meeting Tom for our bike ride together. If, when

----

[1] Both items are on display at Lincolnshire Heritage Aviation Centre, East Kirkby

I had been given that special commemorative mug someone had forecast how it would come to be smashed so few years later I would not have believed them.

The following morning I felt fine, and had a perfectly normal day in the office with no one being aware that anything unusual had occurred the previous evening. There was just one exception to this. One of our WAAF Admin Officers met me in the grounds of the Hall and said "One moment Pickering – I see from the Booking In/Out Book in the Guard Room that you did not sign the book last night. How was that?" I apologised and said that I distinctly remember that I <u>did</u> go into the Guard Room on returning from my evening out – perhaps I had engaged in conversation with someone and so forgot to sign the book? I apologised once again and promised to be more careful in future. Luckily for me I had an unblemished record at Group H.Q., so nothing more was heard of the matter.

Perhaps one day I will drive over to Morton Hall (which is now a Womens' Prison) and see if I can find that pub again but I think it doubtful if I could recognise it after only one visit – and that being nearly sixty years ago.

6. *Tom Joins 463 RAAF Squadron*

As anticipated about a week after "The Bike Ride" took place Tom and the crew, led by the pilot F/O D. G. Tointon, left the Heavy Conversion Unit at R.A.F. Swinderby close by where I was stationed at Morton Hall. On 16th August, 1944 they were posted to 463 Royal Australian Air Force Squadron at R.A.F. Waddington just south of Lincoln to begin their tour of thirty operational sorties flying Lancaster bombers against the enemy before they could expect to be taken off such stressful flying for a "rest" period of instructional duties for about six months.

From reading "Tom and the Bike Ride" you will realise that we had some good times together and that there was a strong bond of friendship between us. I think that in wartime the pace of life was speeded up so tremendously for it might take months or even years in peacetime to get to know someone really well – yet in wartime it often only took days or weeks. Then was not the time to think that if we have a little squabble now we can enjoy "making-up" next time we meet in a few days time. This was particularly true if your boyfriend was aircrew on operational flying, for when one said goodnight and parted after an evening out together, you never knew when or even if the Fates would decree that you ever met again.

I was so pleased that Tom was posted close to Lincoln as this meant we could continue to meet when our off duty times coincided. I believe that at this time I found that Tom was becoming rather possessive, for I see from a letter which Ken wrote to me on 19th September, 1944 that Tom and I were having a "bust-up" because I refused to give up any of my boyfriends. I felt very strongly about this because I greatly valued the friendship of each of them and could not see why I should discard any of them just because Tom wished me to do so. Ken was also on operational flying at this time and I wrote him a daily letter as I had done before to Roo when he was on ops. Both Roo and Ken said they valued this and looked forward to them greatly. No doubt Tom and I continued to meet in Lincoln when he wasn't on ops and, no doubt, he continued to complain that I refused to give up any of my friends for him. By this time Tom would have been on several raids and would have come to realise that his chances of completing a "tour" of 30 ops alive was barely 50/50. Tom was a rear gunner. When flying in the rear turret of a Lanc. it is an incredibly lonely place. One seems to be sitting in space enclosed by a glass bubble of Perspex isolated from the aircraft and the rest of the crew except by intercom for urgent instructions – such as telling the pilot of the approach of enemy fighters. Most raids took place at night and I notice that on Tom's ops the flying time varied tremendously from 3¼ hours to Boulogne and 11¼ hours to Konigsberg. During these long, lonely vigils it must have been good to think that there would be someone awaiting your return to whom your safety would mean everything. A fiancée perhaps? Tom could not have been very pleased that I was planning to go on leave to Edinburgh with Ken. I don't remember that Tom ever referred to the time when he proposed to me over tea at that hotel in Nottingham. Marriage was never mentioned again. Perhaps if I had agreed to having only one boy friend – Tom – things might have been different.

I think that Tom went on leave somewhere between going on a raid to Bremershaven on 18/19th September and a daylight raid to Wilmershaven on 5th October. During his leave he planned to return in time to visit Swinderby again to go to a Sgt's Mess Dance on 23rd September. Tom invited Beryl and me to cycle over the three or four miles to join him there on the other side of the A46 to Morton Hall.

By then I was entitled to go as a fully fledged Corporal – complete with Corporal's stripes – or "tapes" on my arm. But there was a problem! A Corporal or a Sergeant liked to appear to have been holding that rank for a long, long time. Nobody wished to stitch on new "tapes" drawn from the Equipment Section, as their very fresh "newness" would proclaim to the world how new the wearer was to the rank of the tapes displayed.

I tried to find someone who had recently been promoted from Corporal to Sergeant, hoping that I might be able to "scrounge" their old tapes, but I could not find a spare set of well worn tapes anywhere. So, rather than appear in new ones, I went to the Dance in my old rank of LACW.

Tom introduced me to a friend of his, telling him of my recent promotion and he congratulated me and said that when I was "properly dressed" wearing my Cpl's tapes, he would treat me to a meal and a Dance. So, I took him at his word but I said I wanted his offer in writing in case he forgot his promise! He pulled out of his pocket a rather crumpled envelope, removed the letter from it, and wrote on the envelope (which had been addressed to 2225537 Sgt. D. G. J. Price (A/G) c/o Sgts Mess, R.A.F. Swinderby) I PROMISE TO GIVE A DINNER AND DANCE SUPPER when Sylvia gets her <u>tapes</u>. Signed D. G. J. Price, witnessed by B. J. Commin and a name I cannot read. I wonder what happened to him? I doubt whether I am going to be able to redeem that I.O.U. now.

Tom was in a mischievous mood that evening. He noticed that at the end of the room where we were dancing were tables on which were draped two very large flags – the Union Jack and the Australian flag. Tom decided that he wanted to remove the Aussie flag from the table and fly it from the Camp flagpole and egged us on to help him do just that.

First of all we had to get it off the table and out of the building. So we had to stand in front of the table, apparently just in conversation, and gradually ease it off, bit by bit, and fold it up as small as possible before finally managing to smuggle it outside. Beryl and I can still remember what a cold dark night it seemed as Tom led us from the bright lights and warmth of the Mess along pathways in the Camp until we came to the flagpole with its rope halyards eerily rattling in the darkness and chill wind.

Several times we paused when we heard voices and footsteps nearby and I prayed that the Service Police would not discover us. After what seemed an age, Tom eventually hauled his beloved flag to the top of the flagpole, where it was left flying proudly. Thankfully we had not been discovered – it would have been awful if I had been put on a Charge and been demoted to the rank of LACW once again. I would have lost my tapes before I had even got them sewn on!

Once when Beryl Commin was staying with us we were yarning about our time when we were both WAAF clerks at H.Q. 5 Group. I said I wished I knew what the Commanding Officer's reaction was when he discovered the Aussie flag flying. Beryl informed me that the following morning she was told that at the daily morning ceremony of hoisting the Colours to the masthead someone had told the Commanding

Officer of R.A.F. Swinderby that the Aussie flag was already flying there. He said "Why not?" and took no action to find the culprits and it is believed that Tom's beloved Aussie flag remained there all day until the evening ceremony when the Colours were always lowered, removed and the bugler sounded "Sunset".

Barely a fortnight after being posted to Waddington the crew took part in their first operational raid. It was against Konigsberg in East Prussia – a tremendously long trip of nearly 2,000 miles and over eleven hours in duration. Listed on the following pages are the operations of F/O Tointon and his crew as taken from the 463 Operational Record Book. Some details amaze me. On the afternoon of 10th September, 1944 a 4 hour trip to Le Havre (3.30-7.14 p.m.). A short night's sleep because the following day (11th) they took off at 5.16 a.m. for LE HAVRE again, landing at 09.22 (4 hours). There is a second trip <u>on the same day</u> as at 21.05 they took off for DARMSTADT, well into Germany, south of Frankfurt, landing at 02.50 hours after another five hours of operational flying. So between 3.30 p.m. on the 10th September and 3 a.m. on the 12th, three operations were completed involving 13 hours of flying time.

Tom and most of the crew. (Tom is on the right in front row).

Aus. 418890	F/O D. G. Tointon	Pilot
1457829	Sgt. J. P. McLellan	Engineer
Aus. 437332	F/Sgt. D. E. Brown	Navigator
Aus. 426853	F/Sgt. A. Giloran	Bomb Aimer
Aus. 427795	F/Sgt. R. Broad	Wireless Operator
Aus. 439490	F/Sgt. J. MacPherson	Mid Upper Gunner
Aus. 439918	F/Sgt. T. P. Whiteley	Rear Gunner

The crew were all Australians except, as was usual, the Flight Engineer who was in the Royal Air Force.

Extracts from Operational Record Book of No.463 Squadron R.A.A.F.

Date	Target	Up	Down	Duration	Aircraft
29/30 Aug 1944 (Night)	KONIGSBERG (East Prussia)	20.52	07.26	11¼ hrs	Lancaster III. LM683

Crew Report: Sortie completed. Clear over target. Bombing generally appeared to be reasonable.

Op. Log Book: No. 463 Squadron repeated its record trip of 1,850 miles to KONIGSBERG. The aircraft circled the target for twenty-two minutes. The photographs reveal that the bomb load fell in the centre of the town this time, and it is thought that the attack was very successful. 20 aircraft detailed.

Date	Target	Up	Down	Duration	Aircraft
31 Aug (Day)	ROLLENCOURT (N. France Flying Bomb Site)	16.08	20.14	4 hours	Lancaster III. PB 264

Crew Report: Very large explosion at 18.20 hrs following release of bombs.

Op. Log Book Report: Our Squadron made the trip to Northern France to bomb the flying bomb site at ROLLENCOURT. Good aiming point photographs were obtained, and it is believed that it developed and resulted in a very successful attack. 16 aircraft detailed.

Date	Target	Up	Down	Duration	Aircraft
5 Sept (Day)	BREST (French Coast)	16.02	20.25	4½ hours	Lancaster III. LM683

Crew Report: "A" own bursts close. 4 other strikes seen accurate.

Op. Log Book Report: Overcast during morning. Thunderstorm at mid-day. Our Squadron joined in a 5 Group attack on Gun Positions opposite the Port of Brest. Cloud conditions prevented our Air Bombers getting a visual identification of Target, but, considering this, the concentration was very good, and resulted in the immobilisation of several gun positions. 15 Aircraft of this Squadron detailed.

Date	Target	Up	Down	Duration	Aircraft
10 Sept (Day)	LE HAVRE (French Coast)	15.30	19.14	4 hours	Lancaster III. LM 374

Crew Report: Bombing accurate and concentrated.

Op. Log Book Report: Bright sunny day. Our Squadron joined in the attack of freeing the French Port of Le Havre, a much needed Port for transporting of supplies to our troops. The marking was accurate, and it resulted in an excellent concentration which did much to help our troops in the forward area to seize vital defence positions. 20 Aircraft of this Squadron detailed.

Extracts from Operational Record Book of No.463 Squadron R.A.A.F.

Date	Target	Up	Down	Duration	Aircraft
11 Sept (Day)	LE HAVRE (French Coast)	05.16	09.22	4 hours	Lancaster III. LL374

Crew Report: *Bombing well concentrated around markers.*

Op. Log Book Report: *Again the defences of LE HAVRE had a deluge of bombs which appears to have forced them to change their minds, as the Port of LE HAVRE was in our hands 10 hours after this attack. Every crew obtained a most excellent Aiming Point Photograph. 9 aircraft of this Squadron detailed.*

Date	Target	Up	Down	Duration	Aircraft
11/12 Sept 44 (Night)	DARMSTADT (S. of Frankfurt)	21.05	02.50	5¾ hrs	Lancaster III. LM 374

Crew Report: *Sortie completed. Clear over target. Visibility good. 13,750 ft. Bombing seen was really well concentrated around marker. When we left, smoke was nearly up to our height.*

Op. Log Book Report: *Bright sunny day. Our Squadron returned to the attack on DARMSTADT, and caused complete havoc in the town. Fires raging, and smoke rising thousands of feet. Excellent A/P [Aiming Point] photos revealed huge conflagration. 17 Aircraft of this Squadron detailed.*

Date	Target	Up	Down	Duration	Aircraft
17 Sept (Day)	BOULOGNE (French Coast)	08.08	11.18	3¼ hrs	Lancaster III. LM 374

Crew Report: *Bombing looked accurate.*

Op. Log Book Report: *Boys up at 03.00 hours. Take-off 08.00 hrs. Bright sunny day. We joined in attack on German fortress of BOULOGNE a very tenacious bulwark. Good concentration achieved and excellent results obtained. F/O Tanner acquired a hole 11 ft x 7 ft in his wing and made a miraculous landing in an anti-invasion field in France, arriving back here 3 days later. 18 Aircraft of this Squadron detailed.*

Date	Target	Up	Down	Duration	Aircraft
18/19 Sept(Night)	BREMERHAVEN(German Coast)	18.21	23.15	5 hours	Lancaster III. LM 374

Crew report: *Sortie completed. Excellent visibility. Town appeared to be well covered, and all fires could be seen a considerable time on return.*

Op. Log Book Report: *One of the most important ports in N.W. Germany, BREMERHAVEN was the target, and was well marked. A good concentration was achieved. Fires burning in town which could be seen 50 miles on the return journey. Photos revealed fires and smoke. 17 aircraft of this Squadron detailed.*

Extracts from Operational Record Book of No.463 Squadron R.A.A.F.

Date	Target	Up	Down	Duration	Aircraft
5 Oct 44 (Day)	WILHELMSHAVEN (German Coast)	08.25	13.07	5 hours	Lancaster III. LM 374

Crew Report: Sortie completed. 10/10ths cloud – tops about 8,000 ft. Estimated run of 1 minute after crossing coast, ground detail seen.

Op. Log Book Report: Crews called at 01.30 hrs. Take-off delayed 2 hrs. Target WILHELMSHAVEN. This town is the H.Q. of the German Naval Staff, and our Squadron joined with 5 Group on a daylight attack on this target. Cloud was 10/10, and completely obliterated the town. Blind bombing technique was brought into force, and it is thought that the attack was fairly successful. 16 aircraft detailed.

Date	Target	Up	Down	Duration	Aircraft
6 Oct 44 (Night)	BREMEN (N. Germany)	17.40			Lancaster III. LM 374

AIRCRAFT MISSING. NO NEWS AFTER TAKE-OFF

Op. Log Book Report: Bright sunny day. The second largest Port in Germany, Bremen, was "the Target for Tonight". The weather on this occasion was ideal, and our aircraft joined in the attack to set BREMEN on fire. Photographs reveal a huge conflagration of fires over a wide area. Defences were slight, moderate flak with numerous searchlights. Most successful attack. 18 aircraft detailed. Standing by for morning attack.

When I got back to Morton Hall after spending my leave with Ken in Scotland I was shocked to discover that nothing had been heard from Tom and the crew since they took off from Waddington for a raid on Bremen at 17.40 hours on 6th October, 1944 and the crew was listed as "Missing". I don't remember how the awful news came to me or how I managed to get the address of his parents, who were his next of kin. This is a copy of the letter which I sent to them.

R.A.F. Morton Hall
25th October, 1944

Dear Mr. and Mrs. Whiteley,

No doubt you will be surprised to receive a letter from an absolute stranger, but when I returned from Leave and heard that your son was missing I thought I would write to you, as I was lucky to have known Tom since June and valued his friendship.

As I sit here alone by the fire so many thousands of miles away from you, my thoughts reach out in sympathy. Although I could not at first decide whether to write this letter, I felt that you might like to know that although he was so far from his own family and friends, his absence is felt over here with a sense of loss.

I met him and some of the other members of the crew at a Camp Dance shortly before the end of his training. If I remember rightly, we got into some deep and involved discussion upon the rival qualities of Australian and English horseflesh and riding! (As I am very fond of horses I was in my element!)

On another occasion I was lucky enough to have the opportunity of riding in a Gymkhana which was held on the slopes of a wooded hill in the grounds of an old Hall[1] – really delightful settings.

So I invited Tom to come over and see an English Gymkhana in typical "old country" settings. Although it was one of our rare

---

[1] Burton Hall just north of Lincoln

hot days of summer he managed to "hitch hike" over for the afternoon, and I think he quite enjoyed himself.

On these and other occasions I spent some very enjoyable times with him, and always appreciated his never failing cheerfulness and courage.

No matter how fed up with life one might feel, one's gloom was always quickly dispelled by his unfailing good humour.

I hope you will not regard this letter as an intrusion, and will accept my heartfelt sympathy.

I only pray that by the time you receive this letter you will have news that he is safe and well,

Yours sincerely,

Mr. E. J. Whiteley,
44 Waratah Street,
Bexley,
New South Wales,
AUSTRALIA

I did hope that I would receive a reply from Tom's parents to this letter but I heard nothing, which saddened me. Later I was delighted to find that Tom was still alive but a POW.[1] I felt confident that either his parents or Tom himself, via the Red Cross, would contact me. I waited and waited in vain. I then told myself that I must have imagined the bond that I thought there was between us and that I had heard nothing from Tom because I had not meant enough to Tom for him to want to contact me. I knew that at one time he must have thought he loved me as he had asked me to marry him but perhaps that feeling had been merely temporary – a passing

---

[1] Prisoner of war

phase. It never occurred to me that, due to enemy action, mail between us might have gone astray.

Were they missing on their 10th or 11th op? On F/O Tointon's Record Sheet it states that they were on their eleventh op when they were missing on the night of 6th October, 1944 but this seems to be inaccurate in this case. It was usual for the pilot of the new crews on the Squadrons to fly their first op with an experienced crew, as a second pilot. (This was referred to as his "second dickey trip.") This would then count towards the crew's tour of ops. On searching the Operational Record Book pages from 16th August to the end of August, 1944 there is no record of F/O Tointon having made such a trip.

With one exception, of the ten ops reviewed, 15 to 20 aircraft were detailed each time. The Squadron's Operational State on 31.8.44 was Serviceable aircraft: 17, Unserviceable: 2.

Rear Gunner

by the late Ron Smith, DFM[1]

I feared for him
His mind
What he saw
hurtling backwards
to his private war.

He could spare only
a fleeting thought
for the enemy, in the city,
staring up, or hiding from the sound,
of a thousand Merlins
circling round.

When he glanced down
into the target's molten lead,
incinerating the living,
or dead!
suspended four miles high,
in fear and cold
it was retaliation
he's been told.
What words descriptive enough to tell
of a comradeship in hell.
Or explain
what the torment was like
to have to come again, again.
Eight hours or more
is an age – an age!

---

[1] The holder of the copyright of this poem is invited to contact the author of this book.

With only a Perspex capsule
for a stage.

As his friends,
torn asunder in the tortured air
to know only round about
the dank grey clouds,
as shrouds!

On return to base
he couldn't grieve;
or a quiet moment spend,
or really quite believe
the absence of a particular friend
from another crew
who only yesterday he knew,
In any case, it wasn't done.

There are no 'ops' tonight
an evening out instead
may be a twenty-four hour future
lies ahead.
Drink too many beers! Dance!
Find a girl! Laugh! Sing! anything.
To hide that inner mind
already dead.

At times his face
told of a recent leave
normality to retrace,
Not this hideous make believe,
this stark, unreal contrast to home
where there was "sameness",
nothing re-arranged.
In the sudden quietness of his room
staring, dreadful at the papered wall

in his own bed curled
sheltered briefly from that other world
trying the everyday things to recall.

Down the lane,
the old stone school.
Village tea shops, bright awnings
steadfast chapel, Boys brigade,
and breakfast on slow Sunday mornings.

The war took its course
he older, but young in years
still has no tears.
I feared for him more then
for what he saw, now lies
deep, unanswered in his eyes.

Some evenings in the village inn
at times, he heard the idle talk begin,
and at the outside of the crowd
he quietly leaves
and has to be alone,
Hardly speaking, yet not proud
not feeling better than they
because he has hardly anything to say
As he walks, his mind still wanders,
and in so many different ways
living in the memory
of their living days

7. *A Surprise*

In the Spring of 1945 I was hard at work in my office in the
attic of Morton Hall when the telephone rang. Nothing unusual about that. I have never liked the telephone, so I
probably answered without any enthusiasm in my voice but I
was staggered when I discovered who was ringing me from
what sounded like a long distance call. (In those days long
distance calls were usually much less distinct than local
ones). The conversation went something like this:

"Sylvia, is that you?"

"Yes, who is calling, please?"

"Tom, Tom Whiteley!"

"Tom, how absolutely marvellous! Are you O.K? When did
you get back to England?"

"I'm fine – have just landed. How are you? Have you got
engaged to any of those Aussies you were going out with
whilst I have been away?"

"No, but I've got engaged to an Englishman, named
Jimmy, who is also an Air Gunner".

I can't remember much more of the conversation after
that.

As I had had no contact with Tom since before he took off
on that fateful flight on 6th October, '44 it took me completely by surprise when he telephoned me as soon as he was
back in England saying he wanted to see me again despite
the fact that I told him I was now engaged to Jimmy. Perhaps,
in all those horrible months in a dreaded P.O.W. camp he had

spent a lot of time thinking about the fun times we had had together and had hoped that they would be resumed on his eventual return to this country. I don't know. It was arranged that Beryl and I would meet him and his friend in Lincoln. His companion was probably a crew member who had been a P.O.W. with him.

I see from an old unfinished letter to Gladys Rogers (a WAAF friend whom I had met at Cottesmore in January 1941) that I got engaged to Jimmy in March 1945. Therefore, at that time I would have been full of excitement over my recent engagement party at Jimmy's home near Reading and our plans to get married a few months later, so I don't suppose my thoughts were very much on Tom. When Beryl and I met Tom again I vaguely wondered why he did not seem quite the same as I had remembered him. Beryl says he did say he had had a very gruelling time on a forced march as a P.O.W. I did not remember his saying this, or it may be that I did not take in what he said because I was so enamoured of Jimmy. How blind I must have been not to have taken in the fact that it was amazing that Tom was able to be there at all. If I had known then the full horrific details of the forced march that alone would have left barely healed scars, both mentally and physically forever, without even taking into consideration the trauma of the crash when three of his fellow crew members were killed. He had only just returned to England from all those tragic events and I was stupid enough to wonder why he did not seem quite the same as when we last met intent on removing the Aussie flag to fly it from the flagpole during the Sergeant's Mess dance at Swinderby! They say that love is blind. I was in love with Jimmy. Therefore I was blind. What other excuse can I give? Mea culpa.

When Tom realised that I could not be persuaded to go back to him, he said he would take the lengthy leave to which he was entitled and go over to visit Ireland, as he believed he had some relatives there. Naturally I hoped that Tom would enjoy his leave in Ireland and I looked forward to my marriage to Jimmy and so we parted.

Sadly my happy state of euphoria about my engagement and forthcoming marriage to Jimmy did not last long. At first I was greatly relieved when my engagement to Jimmy was at an end as I was sure that we would not have been suited to spend a life time together – for in those far off days it was rare to contemplate divorce.

After these initial feelings of relief were over I felt lonely and much in need of someone to confide in to comfort and support me. Who could I turn to? I was an only child and my mother was dead and my father would not have understood why I was unhappy. I believed Roo to be dead. Ken would have tried his best to make me happy again but I dare not let him know how I felt as that would have raised his hopes that perhaps one day I might change my mind and agree to marry him.

My thoughts turned to Tom. I had heard nothing from him since we parted and he went to Ireland on a long repatriation leave to look up relatives there.

I now tried to find out where Tom was so that I could contact him but I could hardly believe the news that I gleaned on the "grape vine". On his leave Tom had met and married a very quiet, shy Irish girl! This meant that I dared not look to Tom for friendship and support as he was now a married man. My earlier friendship with Roo[1] had given me painful

---

[1] Roo – the story of Roo is in my previous book

experience of how difficult it can become to control one's feelings as they may develop into something stronger and deeper than was originally intended.

In the Autumn, when all the brides of the Aussies had been collected together to wait for a ship to take them to the other side of the world to their future homes in Australia, I heard that Tom's young wife was still so shy that she stayed in her room and would not come out to mix with the other young brides with whom she would be sailing for so many weeks to a country so different to her native Ireland to live with a man she had known for such a short period of time. Perhaps it was an attraction of opposites. Perhaps it was that rare occurrence – love at first sight. Whatever it was, I do so hope they were happy together for I was very fond of Tom. I loved his kind, strong character and ever cheerful extrovert nature.

8. *Jimmy*

Christmas 1944 was my fourth spent in the WAAF. After various trials and tribulations over the years I had become a Corporal and now had one or two minor privileges such as a little more pay and membership of the Corporals' Club. I was now in charge of a hut of shift workers. Therefore, I was free to come and go from it more or less when I chose without having an N.C.O. to query my comings and goings.

I think I may have been feeling somewhat restless as I had a shortage of "serious" boyfriends at that time. It was almost two years since I last saw Roo at my mother's funeral in February 1943 and I did not know whether he was dead or alive. Tom and his crew never returned from a trip to Bremen on the night of 6th October, 1944. To use an Aussie expression Ken and I were still great "mates" but I did not love him. So perhaps that is why I fell in love with Jimmy – the determined strong-willed one who turned up at one of the little dances at Group when there was an emptiness in my heart. I don't know.

It is very strange. Although Jimmy and I became officially engaged and planned to get married not long afterwards, I remember less about him than I do about Roo, Tom or Ken. I have needed the following extracts from an unfinished letter I wrote to a WAAF friend from my days at Cottesmore, Gladys Rogers, on 5th March, 1946 a couple of months after I had been demobbed, to have any idea of dates at all:

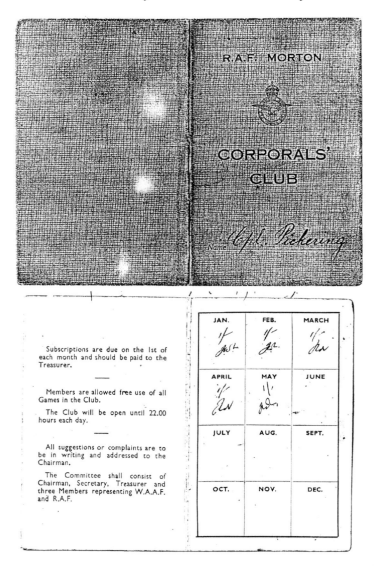

Corporals' Club Membership Card

Jimmy

"I am glad to hear your good news re settling down permanently, but you don't sound 100% keen about it. A year ago last Christmas Eve (December 1944) I met an awfully nice boy – Jimmy a Sgt. A/G[1] (civvy street Radio Diagnostician at Marconi). We got engaged in March, nearly married in September, and broke it off in November. For heavens sake don't marry him unless you do really feel you want to spend the next 50 odd years with him and no one else! Listen to Granny – the old bind!"

How attitudes towards marriage have changed since I wrote that letter to Gladys over fifty years ago! I wonder why I never finished the letter but I did have a piece wedding cake sent to

---

[1] Air Gunner

me from her home in Middlesborough and I hope all went well with them both.

To return to Jimmy. Like Tom before him Jimmy was finishing his training at R.A.F. Swinderby Heavy Conversion Unit before the start of operational flying.

Jimmy had a lovely little red M.G. sports car which was his pride and joy but little used due to the very strict petrol rationing. I used to joke and say that I didn't need a nail file any more because I could just sit and trail my fingers on the road as he drove along as we were so close to the ground that I could file my nails in that way! I remember being very impressed – but rather unbelieving – when Jimmy told me that at Marconi plans were afoot to make gramophone records out of date as, in the future, music and speech would be recorded on some sort of wire or tapes – shades of things to come!

I don't remember how Jimmy used to cross the few miles from R.A.F. Swinderby to R.A.F. Morton Hall, as it certainly wasn't on a bus route. Nevertheless I clearly remember very many lengthy "good-nights" to each other in January 1945, standing in brilliant moonlight beneath some old Scots Pine trees at the edge of Morton Hall grounds with the temperature well below freezing, gradually becoming colder and colder. First the feet froze, then the legs up to the knees and so on... We used to say to each other that Paradise must be where we would be in a warm bed together and not have to part to go to our chilly Nissen huts miles apart! I was very thankful that by then I was the N.C.O. in charge of my hut so that there would be no one to query the hour at which I returned to my bed. There was an iron stove in the centre of the hut and as the occupants were shift workers there was usually some degree of warmth still left in it, no matter what time of night it was. This helped in the thawing-out process although it was not unusual for one's feet still to be icy cold when it was time to get up again a few hours later.

I see from the unfinished letter to Gladys that we planned to get married in September. Why then? Perhaps Jimmy hoped to have completed his tour of thirty ops by then? I wonder where we were going to get married? My Mother had died a couple of years before and my Father, who was in his mid seventies (he was twenty years older than my Mother) would not have had the interest or ability to cope with arranging a wedding.

When Jimmy and I were making plans I believe I wrote to one of the top film studios based near London to ask if I could hire one of the wedding dresses used in one of their films as, due to clothes rationing and being in the Forces, I should have been hard put to it to have obtained a suitable gown for the white wedding we planned.

When Jimmy and the crew had finished their training at the Heavy Conversion Unit at R.A.F. Swinderby they were posted far away to north-east Lincolnshire to begin operational flying from R.A.F. Strubby. Jimmy provided me with this copy of a note he had left in his kit in case he did not return.

Jimmy's Hand written Note

Soon after this posting he developed numbness and an increasing lack of feeling in one of his legs. He was admitted to Louth Hospital, high up on the Lincolnshire Wolds in the north-east of the county. I remember spending a day off trying to get over to Louth to visit him and walking up a long steep hill to find the hospital. When at last I found him in bed he was very worried as he understood that he would be facing a dangerous operation which, if not successful, could leave him paralysed. I think it had something to do with a trapped nerve in the spine. I believe that in those days any operations on the spine had very considerable risks attached to them – no doubt these days, for aught I know, they may be done routinely.

I was feeling very depressed as I made my way back across the county to Morton Hall, as I found the prospect of marrying a young man who might be confined to a wheel chair for the rest of his life, perhaps fifty years, very daunting. Nevertheless, even if this did happen, I still planned to go ahead with our wedding. Due to the fact that Jimmy had to face this major operation all the plans for the actual date of our wedding were held over until after the operation and whatever period of time was needed for his convalescence.

Jimmy had the operation at R.A.F. Hospital, Rauceby, near Sleaford. Thankfully it was a complete success and I used to have almost a daily letter from him there. I still have his envelopes date stamped as follows:

24 May 45	30 May 45	7 Jun 45	30 Aug. 45
(10.15 a.m.)	31 May 45	16 Aug. 45	31 Aug. 45
24 May 45	1 Jun 45	22 Aug. 45	4 Sept 45
(5.15 p.m.)	4 Jun 45	23 Aug. 45	11 Sept 45
25 May 45	5 Jun 45	28 Aug. 45	13 Sept 45
27 May 45	6 Jun 45	29 Aug. 45	

I can only imagine that the May/June group was written when he went to Rauceby for investigation and the second group after the operation had taken place. I just don't know for sure.

Envelope dated 4th June, 1945

Now, holding these envelopes in my hand, I feel sad to think that at some stage in my life I decided that the envelopes meant more to me than the love letters they had once contained, for I still have the envelopes but they are all empty. Perhaps this is because of my life long love of stamp collecting which started as a child through a clergyman uncle of mine who gave me a mixed packet of 500 stamps and a Woolworth's Stamp Album when I was at home with measles, mumps or some other childhood ailment. The interest he nurtured in philately (he had a fine collection which I subsequently inherited) continued even during the war years. So, after V.E. Day, when the stamps were franked with a pair of bells and a "V" sign to celebrate Victory in Europe, I saved all such envelopes that came my way. That is why I still have those envelopes even though they are empty for my love of philately lasted longer than my love for Jimmy.

Eventually Jimmy was sent to a large house in the depths of the countryside to convalesce. I have no idea where it was but I do know I had great difficulty in "hitching" a lift to visit him as it was nowhere near bus or train routes. I think that by then I had begun to have doubts about our suitability for a lifetime together. I had put any such thoughts to the back of my mind before Jimmy had his operation because I wished to give him all the support possible and I did not want it to look as if I was backing out of our engagement because I could not face being married to a man who was confined to a wheel-chair. Now, thankfully, Jimmy expected to be O.K. after his convalescence although unfit for flying duties.

At this country house convalescent home we were alone together in an upstairs room, sitting on his bed and enjoying a kiss and a cuddle. Suddenly I was aware of hoof beats below the window and, wanting to see what was going on, I deter-minedly pulled away from Jimmy despite his protests and went over to the window to have a look. Jimmy was furious and we had our first – and last – huge row. At the end of it we were no longer engaged to be married.

I quite thought that Jimmy would write to me; that we would both say we were sorry for losing our tempers; things would be sorted out and all would be well. I thought wrongly. I never had any contact at all with Jimmy after that day. He did not write, telephone or even send a message. Perhaps I should have been warned by what Jimmy wrote on the two photos of himself which he gave me. On one was written in French "Love no one but me". On the other "Nemo me impune lacessit" (No one hurts me with impunity). I believe it is the motto of Scotland. Whether or not the origins of his surname are in Scotland I do not know or whether it was a warning about his character which I failed to heed, I also do not know.

After a suitably lengthy period of time, when it seemed that it was no good waiting any longer for Jimmy to contact me, I sent back the engagement ring with the emerald in it. I had been advised not to have an emerald in my engagement ring as they were unlucky but did not believe the superstition. Nevertheless, perhaps emeralds weren't unlucky for me as I think it is fortunate that the engagement was broken off when it was as, looking back, I am sure that we were both too fiery and immature to have made the marriage work.

Eventually Jimmy's mother wrote to me to say that the ring had reached Jimmy safely; she was very sorry that our engagement was at an end and that Jimmy was very hurt by my breaking things off and returning the ring.

This made me feel just a wee bit guilty so, at a later date I spent a leave with my Aunt and Uncle in Reading, so that I could call "casually" at Jimmy's home a few miles away to enquire about his well-being. His mother opened the door to me, did not invite me into the house but said that Jimmy was well and had returned to his previous job with Marconi. Our conversation together was quite brief and without warmth on her part, nevertheless I was very thankful to be assured that Jimmy was well and back working at his old job.

Now I knew for certain that Jimmy and I had permanently parted I was totally unprepared for the wonderful feeling of relief and freedom which swept over me, in fact, when I returned from my leave, for the first time ever, I often found myself humming as I went about my duties. It was a popular song written by Cole Porter and sung by Bing Crosby and the Andrews Sisters entitled "Don't Fence Me In"! The words seemed to express my feelings then:

"Oh give me land, lots of land and starry skies above,
Let me ride through the wide open country that I love,
DON'T FENCE ME IN!

Let me be myself in the evening breeze,
Listen to the murmur in the cottonwood trees
DON'T FENCE ME IN!

Let me gaze at the moon until I lose my senses,
Send me off forever, but I ask you please –
DON'T FENCE ME IN!

Let me ride to the ridge where the west commences,
I can't look at hobbles and I can't stand fences –
DON'T FENCE ME IN!

Just turn me loose, let me straddle my old saddle
Underneath the western skies –
On my cayuse let me wander over yonder
Till I see the mountains rise
DON'T FENCE ME IN!

After Jimmy and I had split up I was surprised when my WAAF friends said that they had not thought we were suited to each other and were quite pleased that we were no longer "an item" as they would term it these days! I had no idea they thought this whilst Jimmy and I were going out together – perhaps the old saying "that onlookers see most of the game" is a true saying?

9. *Two's Company*

I met Jimmy on Christmas Eve 1944 and we became engaged in March 1945, so it was very likely in February of that year that I thought it would be a good idea to take Jimmy home to meet my father. He was still living in our home at Saxilby with an R.A.F. Officer and his wife from R.A.F. Scampton, about ten miles away, who shared the house.

We were not on the telephone at home and my father and I did not write to each other. I can only once remember receiving a letter from him during my five years in the WAAF. So my father had no idea that Jimmy and I were turning up for the weekend. I did not expect any problems because "White Lodge" had four bedrooms – one for my father, another for the R.A.F. Officer and his wife, the third for me and the fourth, which used to be the maid's bedroom, up the open-tread stairs to the attic, I anticipated Jimmy could use.

So far, so good. Jimmy left R.A.F. Swinderby, I left Morton Hall and we both went into Lincoln. In due course we caught Hutson's hourly bus service out to Saxilby together and walked up the driveway of White Lodge in the darkness of winter and blackout. On opening the front door we entered the dimly lit hall. Despite the low lighting I was taken aback to see the unmistakable dark blue of an Aussie greatcoat hanging on a peg on the hall coat-stand. Ken must be staying! Ken was at R.A.F. Binbrook, high up on the Lincolnshire Wolds. Ken used to get on well with my father and so was at liberty to go and stay at "White Lodge" whenever he was free from operational flying and in need of a break. What on earth should I do now?

Fortunately I had always been completely honest with my boyfriends and they all knew of each other's existence – and I had promised them never to have more than six at one time – which included those who were in this country and those posted abroad. Therefore, Ken and Jimmy knew of each other but neither they nor I expected them to meet. Suddenly I felt as if I were a tempting juicy bone over which two fit and hungry dogs were liable to quarrel openly at any moment.

When introductions were over, Ken immediately said that *he* would leave so that Jimmy could have the spare bed. Jimmy said *he* would leave as Ken was already a guest in the house. Whilst they were arguing about who should leave, I remember grabbing Ken's greatcoat from the coat-stand in the hall, dashing with it into the darkness outside and hiding it in Bridget's stable down the garden path, as I knew that Ken needed the break from flying on ops more than Jimmy, who had not yet begun operational flying.

I frantically hoped that the three of us would be joined by my father and that, despite the odds, all would yet be well. It wasn't. My father had arranged for a neighbouring couple to come round and play Bridge that evening. He did not wish his foursome to be disturbed by anyone else in the room. The R.A.F. Officer and his wife had the use of the other sitting room (although I don't think they were in that evening). So that left the Breakfast Room as the only place where the three of us could sit in relative comfort.

Imagine the scene. A dark cold winter's night, in a house in a country village in wartime. Blackout; no street lighting; strict fuel rationing. No spare food or drink for entertaining unexpected guests – or even expected ones due to strict rationing – which was far worse for civilians than for those of us in the Forces as we had so many Canteens open to us. No television or videos for entertainment. No record player and the only wireless (radio) was in the room where my Father was playing Bridge. What could I do with them both? They wouldn't be pleasantly conversational. They did not want to play cards. "Happy Families" would certainly not have fitted the bill that night! I didn't enjoy the next hour or two. In the past I had felt quite safe in saying to Jimmy, if he had annoyed me in some way "Ken would never have said/done that!" and vice versa. Now, here they were face to face and each as grumpy and irritable as the other and not living up to the glowing character I had given each to the other.

I then remembered that Jimmy was musical and managed to find my mother's mandolin and/or banjo to keep him occupied. I found some skeins of wool and asked Ken to hold them for me so that I could then wind them into balls. These must have been a legacy from my mother as I have rarely ever knitted – it always took me a full year of toil to knit even a sleeveless pullover. I think it was finally decided that Ken should continue his stay, as I don't remember retrieving his greatcoat. Time seemed to pass incredibly slowly but at last I think it was Jimmy who went out to catch Hutson's bus back into Lincoln once again. I don't know where he planned to spend the night. I do know that I spent until about 2 p.m. the following day with one of them and then changed over for the remainder of the day and evening with the other one.

So, any girls reading this, remember, honesty is the best policy. I could rightly have been accused of "two-timing" at the very least and would have lost the trust, if not the friendship, of both of them. As it was, all's well that ended well.

10. *My "Cook's Tour"*

When we were very young I am sure most of us held secret dreams as to what we would like to happen when we "grew up". I was no exception. I had two wishes. One was that I should have my own mare, breed from her and school and ride her offspring myself. This I have been able to do more than once.

The other ambition I never realised – I wanted to own and pilot my own aircraft. You must remember that in the days when I was young (1930s) it was long before flying abroad for summer holidays in the sun was normal practice for thousands of people as it is now. You had to be rich to fly.

I believe that, occasionally, (Sir) Alan Cobham brought his "Flying Circus" to the West Common at Lincoln and on these occasions the public could pay 5/- (25p) for a short flight in an elderly biplane. Even if I could have afforded a flight I doubt if my parents would have given their consent for me to do such a "risky thing!"

Anyway, I had no cash to spare for such "flights of fancy" as it was all I could do to scrape enough money together to keep my pony, Peter, (predecessor of Bridget) as his grazing cost five shillings per week and I only got 6d (2½p) per week pocket money from my father plus another 6d for mowing both the front and back lawns with the old push mower – no labour saving motorised lawn mowers in those days. When the caterpillars were busy devouring the cabbages I could earn an extra penny for each fifty that I destroyed and a similar amount for removing daisies from either lawn. They soon became virtually extinct as my father usually discovered them first and dug them out with the blade of an old kitchen knife. I regularly used to play croquet with my father on the back lawn for a penny a game to the winner. That was expensive for me too, for although I was allowed some bisques[1] as he was the better player, I usually lost most of my pocket money back to him each week. Grazing in a field for Pete cost 5/- (25p) per week and the blacksmith charged 5/- for a set of new shoes for him (Bridget's feet were a little larger so her shoes cost 6/- for a set.) Therefore all Birthday and Christmas money received from friends and relations went on their upkeep.

It was not until I had my first job, which was at the R.A.F. Recruiting Centre at Newport Barracks in Lincoln and my first wages (£2 10s. per week[2]), that I could afford the unaccustomed pleasure of buying a Mars Bar, or something similar, every day for lunch! However, this was a short-lived luxury, for no sooner had I got used to this daily treat than sweet rationing was introduced which put a stop to it.

I have no idea why flying interested me so much. I used to read "Flight" and "Popular Flying" in Lincoln Public Library. At Boarding School at Ambleside, in the Lake District, the pupils in my Form had to choose a subject and give a twenty minute talk on it. I chose "The History of Flight" and illustrated my talk with the aid of an epidiascope. How bored my fellow classmates must have been! I well remember going to Bainbridges (or was it Mawer and Collinghams[3]) department

----

[1] extra turns

[2] £2.50

[3] Now Binns department store

store in Lincoln with my mother to choose a new winter coat. One was almost exactly Air Force blue in colour. Despite my mother favouring a different garment, I eventually had the one of my choice without giving away my secret that it was only the colour which made me choose it. I was far too shy to admit that to anyone. When I stayed with relations at Leadenham I used to ride several miles to a field on the High Dyke near Cranwell to watch the budding pilots flying Hawker Harts and Hinds over a field bordering the grassy track of the old Roman Ermine Street. Sometimes they flew very low over us which was very upsetting for the young three year old horse that I had borrowed.

I was thrilled to read about the formation of the WAAF and I longed to be able to enlist and eventually I was old enough and began my WAAF life on 1st January, 1941. However, it was not until shortly after V.E. Day that my chance to fly came about. At that time I was at R.A.F. Morton Hall near Lincoln. On a Notice Board was pinned a statement that some WAAFs would be permitted to fly over Germany in a Lancaster to see the bomb damage. Numbers were strictly limited and we were to sign the list if we wished to fly and would be told at a later date whether or not our application was successful.

Because Thomas Cook was the initiator of holidays abroad "to see the sights" these flights became known as "Cook's Tours". I was delighted when I found that my name was on the list of those permitted to fly – provided that we could first survive a flight in a small two-seater biplane to test whether or not we were likely to be airsick on the long flight over the North Sea to Germany and back in the Lancaster. I knew full well that this would be a difficult test for me as I always had to sit in the front seat of a bus or car or I soon felt sick. On a rare visit to a fairground on its annual visit to Lincoln two of the lesser stomach-churning rides were all I could stand without feelings of nausea coming over me. However, I was absolutely determined that I was going to fly in that Lanc – come what may.

It was a lovely warm sunny day when a group of us were taken over to R.A.F. Swinderby for our trial flight. I thoroughly enjoyed flying over my home town of Lincoln and seeing the Cathedral from the air and all the little houses around about. Nevertheless, by the time we landed at Swinderby again, I was feeling very sick. The WAAF Officer in charge of us asked how I felt and I replied "Fine, Ma'am, just fine". Luckily I was able to make my escape to the long fresh green grass and tall cow parsley at the base of a friendly hedge and hid in its shade until I had recovered sufficiently to be able to join the rest of the group to go back to Morton Hall. No one had discovered my guilty secret – my chances of going on a flight in a Lanc were good!

The list went up on the Notice Board of those who were permitted to take the flight. Thankfully, mine was on it.

We were to fly from nearby R.A.F. Skellingthorpe, which was a Bomber Station opened in November 1941 among the birch woods on the southern edge of Lincoln, where Birchwood housing estate now covers much of the area. As it was after V.E. Day[1] there was no need to have a full crew on the Lanc as there was no danger of enemy attack. A lorry from R.A.F. Skellingthorpe collected us from Group and ferried us back to Skellingthorpe where an Aussie crew member took us over to the Parachute Section to be fitted with parachutes before our flight. I was quite surprised to find how heavy they

----

[1] Victory in Europe Day

were and uncomfortable to walk in. I was so pleased that we were to be with an Aussie crew or part of one. (Ted Richardson tells me we might have flown with 467 Squadron of which he was a member as they did fill in a short time there doing such tours for WAAFs.)

Two WAAF were to fly in each aircraft and I was paired up with a girl whom I had never met but I did not have a chance to talk to her because she chose to go down into the Bomb Aimer's compartment with a book and I did not see her again until we landed.

As Roo, my Aussie friend of 97 Squadron, had been an Observer (Navigator) I chose to sit at the Navigator's table as my base and visualised to myself how he must have sat so often in a similar position but in very different conditions.

As we flew eastwards towards the coast it was quite chilly and cloudy. Then we flew higher through patches of warm bright sunshine and then back again through thick chilly cloud – I was surprised how immediately one felt such a great change in temperature between when flying in full sun and the damp "foggy" cloud. We then flew for quite a long time over the North Sea in bright hot sunshine with the thick clouds spread out beneath us like a grubby grey carpet, obscuring the sea below. I was fascinated and it reminded me of going for a walk in a school "crocodile" up the steep Kirkstone Pass in fog and we suddenly got above it and saw the peaks of the Lake District mountains poking through it and we were in bright sunshine. I remember thinking at the time "so this is what it must be like to be flying above the clouds."

In those peaceful far off days at Ambleside it would have been impossible to have imagined that the next time I was in sunshine above the clouds, although I should still be wearing a uniform, it would not be a school one and the aircraft which was transporting me had never taken part in carrying passengers to eagerly awaited holidays abroad for relaxation in the sun. I digress.

After a time the heat from the sun was so great that it was like sitting in a greenhouse on a hot summer's day, so it was suggested that I discard my parachute. It was certainly much more comfortable without it and I could move about the aircraft more easily.

In due course, by dint of hand signals, as the noise of the engines was so great that communication by speech was virtually impossible, I was invited to go and stand by the pilot and look down below as we were approaching the Friesian Islands. They appeared to be flat and grassy, dotted with farmhouses and with numerous black and white dairy cows which took their breed name from those islands and are now commonly seen in this country too. On hearing the approach of the aircraft everyone rushed out to wave a welcome to us or waved brightly coloured towels out of upstairs windows – they were all obviously delighted to see a Lancaster of the Royal Air Force. By then we seemed to be flying so low and just skimming over the hedges that the cows were fleeing with their tails in the air – I guess their milk output was low for a few days afterwards or, perhaps even curdled! I thought "Oh, Lordy, Lordy, I haven't got my parachute on". Then quickly told myself not to be so stupid – we were flying far too low for a parachute to be of use even if anything did go wrong.

Having "done" the Friesian Islands we then flew north for quite a long time and I returned to sit at the Navigator's table as there was little to see except the sea, as all the fog had dispersed earlier.

After some time had elapsed, and as we were flying straight and level, I thought it would be a good opportunity to venture down the fuselage to see what it was like to sit in the Rear Gunner's turret, as my mate Tom Whiteley occupied such a place on ops. Having received permission to do this, I laboriously climbed up and over the main spar and eventually managed to reach the gun turret which seemed to be swinging about a bit on its axis but I eventually managed to get inside it and sit down. It was very cold and draughty but I had a superb all-round view. I almost felt detached from the rest of the world – as if I were sitting in a soap bubble suspended in space with the earth spread out below me like a map. A truly amazing sensation although a very lonely place it seemed to me.

Unfortunately when I got to the gun turret the timing coincided with our arrival at Heligoland for we immediately flew round and round that beastly island, first on one wing tip and then on the other, at varying heights until the crew became, presumably, bored by their antics and flew straight and level once more. After a period of level flight I thought longingly for the comparative comfort of the Navigator's table and seat as, not surprisingly, I was feeling very sick indeed from my airborne gyrations.

On my return journey the distance from the tail to the main spar seemed to have trebled and it took a great effort to climb up and over it again. I had planned to call in at the Mid Upper Gun Turret position on my way back up the fuselage to the Navigator's table, as my Aussie mate Ken of 460 R.A.A.F. Squadron at Binbrook was a mid Upper Gunner. However, it looked such a tricky climb up into it that I felt such clambering would be the "last straw" for my heaving stomach and, above all, I dare not risk being sick over the crew's beloved

Lanc – this was not a peacetime holiday flight when all passengers were automatically issued with "sick bags". Thankfully I reached the Navigator's table at last and I sank down on the seat, resting my head on my folded arms on the table to try to recover my composure and let my churning insides settle down.

It had been intended to fly down the infamous Ruhr valley which the R.A.F. had visited so many times with terrible losses, but once we had reached land the fog became increasingly thick. One of the crew motioned me to go forwards and then look down towards the fog enshrouded earth below, shouting out what memorable sight it was that we had flown all this way to see but his words were drowned by the steady roar of our Merlin engines and I have no idea of our exact position or what I should have seen if the fog had not been there. We continued like this for a while but the fog showed no sign of lifting, so the rest of our "Cook's Tour" was aborted and we headed for home.

By the time we were flying across the North Sea again all the fog had cleared and we were flying in sunshine once more but with a layer of cloud below us obscuring our view of the sea. We made no exciting detours on our way back, merely flew steadily, straight and level all the way. For which I was devoutly thankful. So by the time we landed again at R.A.F. Skellingthorpe I was feeling much better. The other WAAF reappeared from the Bomb Aimer's position, clutching her book, presumably refreshed after several hours of reading and dozing. On getting out of the aircraft I was asked by a WAAF Officer how I felt. I said "Fine, Ma'am, just fine". An Aussie voice drawled "She was as green as the graaass". True, but it was one of the most memorable days of my life – memories which I still treasure to this day.

11. *V.E. Day and After*

I have read numerous accounts of wonderful celebrations and parties which took place on V.E. Day[1] but regretfully admit to having no such memories myself. I think I spent the day in the office as usual. Being extremely tired went to bed in my hut at an early hour and slept very heavily. The following day I heard all about the "goings-on" which had taken place in Lincoln and was very sorry to have missed it all. So Beryl and I decided to go into Lincoln that evening to join in the jollifications but we found the City was as flat as yesterday's champagne. We were too late. I don't even remember V.J. Day[2] taking place at all.

For those last few months of 1945 I felt very restless and unsettled as now I had no goal at which to aim. For nearly five years the whole purpose of my life in the WAAF had been targeted at trying to help defeat the enemy and to avoid becoming another subjugated slave nation, with all the horrors that would have entailed. Against tremendous odds and at great cost in human lives, this had now been accomplished and we had great hopes for a peaceful and happier future. Whilst we were all involved in fighting for our very freedom it was natural to work as hard as possible to "win the war".

----

[1] 8th May, 1945

[2] 2nd September, 1945

Air / Intelligence Staffs H.Q., No. 5 Group R.A.F. – April 1945

(from left) Front row: (7th) Air Vice-Marshal H.A. Constantine CBE, DSO; (5th) Lt-Col Frank Russell. Second row: (6th) Group Photographic Officer; (7th) S/Ldr Philip T. Bowcock. Third row: (8th) Cpl Sylvia Pickering.

Now that V.E. and V.J. Days were over I no longer found it possible to feel the same way about life in the WAAF as it had, for me at least, more or less lost its purpose. Therefore, minor WAAF rules and regulations became more and more irksome. I wanted "OUT". Presumably I was asked if I wanted to stay on in the WAAF and be posted abroad as a number of girls did so and went on to serve in Europe and the Middle East. I have been told that there were numerous classes available for those who had chosen to be demobbed but I do not remember anything about them at all – I certainly did not attend any.

I had been Clerk to the Station Defence Officers from November 1943 but no longer were Lancasters leaving our 5 Group airfields night after night on raids. No longer had my two Defence Officers the need to secure the defence of those airfields against enemy attack. We had become redundant. My two bosses, Lt. Col. Frank Russell and S/Ldr Philip T. Bowcock, could find little work to keep me occupied. So a huge box of Amendment Lists to various R.A.F. Publications was brought out of hiding from the shelves in the big walk-in stationery cupboard for me to cut out and stick in the various amendments as appropriate – just as I had been doing for a time at R.A.F. Cottesmore in 1941/42 when there was a lull in my work load. I think the three of us knew full well that this was just a ploy to keep me occupied!

From 25th October, 1945 I had a chit certifying that I was "permitted to wear plain clothes when not on duty and off camp".

S/Ldr Bowcock was shortly to return to his peacetime occupation as a solicitor in Leek, Staffordshire and he invited me to join his office staff when I was demobbed. However, I declined his kind offer as, although I both liked and respected him and was very happy when we worked together up in our attic offices at Morton Hall, I felt that things would be very different if I went to work for him at Leek where his own office staff would be very unlikely to welcome an ex-WAAF "outsider" into their closely knit circle. Our relationship would be quite different in peacetime – he would no longer be "my" boss, I should have to share him with his peacetime office staff and I should have felt that I was an interloper.

At the beginning of November I was given the following instructions:

INSTRUCTIONS FOR
DEFENCE SECTION CLERK – COL PICKERING
Period mid-day 6.Nov.45 – Mid-day 15.Nov.45.

--o0o--

1.   You will be attached to the office of Org.I. for the period mid-day 6th of November to mid-day 15th November inclusive, and will report to S/Ldr. Williams, Org.I. at 1430 hours on the 6th.

2.   You will collect daily by 0930 hours any defence mail or signals and report the same and subject to S/Ldr. Pugh, Scampton 56.   There is no need to send Nil returns.   The correspondence should be left in the "IN" tray in the stationery cupboard.

3.   You will contact P.2. Clerk daily to see if there are any instructions for Col. Russell from either Bomber Command or Army Headquarters and send them on by telephone to Pollards 4921.

6th November, 1945.

                                          LT.COL.
                                          G.D.O.

(5G/1416/3/Def)

I had believed this would be a brief absence as we never said goodbye but I did not see either of them again. A few years later S/Ldr Bowcock wrote and asked if I had had news of the Colonel as he had lost touch with him after the Colonel had been posted to Germany.

Now there was no work for me to do except write personal letters and put crumbs near the skirting board for the wee mouse who had nibbled a hole through into my office. I also put crumbs out through the skylight for the birds. As the roof was steeply sloping I don't know whether any remained on the roof or whether they were all blown away. Nevertheless I did my best.

I had no idea what the future held in store for me. I was equally qualified to earn my living with horses as in an office. I knew that earning a living with horses was physically very hard work and poorly paid compared with a good secretarial job, nevertheless I felt a need to get away from an office, at least for a time.

Since my Mother's untimely death in February 1943 my elderly Father had remained living in the family home. An R.A.F. Officer and his wife from R.A.F. Scampton continued to share the house with him but I realised they would soon be leaving now the war had ended. When demobbed I decided to go home for the time being, spend my time riding and looking after my father. I thought that I might then seek my fortune in London as a bi-lingual secretary (French and German) as there were plenty of jobs there and the pay was particularly good.

My social life had ended as my Aussie boyfriends had returned to their homeland, so Beryl and I used to go to the NAAFI Club in Lincoln as there was nothing to do at Group H.Q. We became friendly with two aircrew members of a Polish Lancaster Squadron who were based to the north of Lincoln. I had a great admiration for the Poles and a tremendous feeling of sadness for all the terrible sufferings of their people when their country was overrun by the enemy. They were certainly indomitable fighters. Beryl partnered Wolf – who gave the impression that he might well live up to the English translation of the name, whilst his much quieter friend, Henryk, became my partner.

Henryk

By then there was a very comfortable newly built NAAFI Club in Lincoln near Mint Street and I think we spent most of our spare time there, eating and chatting. I don't remember dancing with either of them or going to the cinema although Henryk and I went to a cinema in Lincoln High Street to enjoy a piano recital by the well-known Rawicz and Landauer.

Eventually the date for my demobilisation was given out – 8th January, 1946. Before this I planned to use up all the Leave due to me, which included time over Christmas with my relations at Leadenham and I had planned to go there on the 20th December.

So I arranged a little "farewell party" for the four of us to take place at the Grand Hotel in Lincoln on the night of the 19th/20th. Beryl, Wolf, Henryk and I would make up a foursome for dinner and a bed for the night was booked for Beryl and myself. Here follows part of a letter I wrote to Ted Richardson on 27th December 1994 about my memorable "farewell party"

As you were kind enough to say that you liked the brief details of my demob party, here – for the first time in print – is the unexpurgated version!

You may remember that Beryl and I had booked in at the Grand Hotel for the night of 19th/20th December, and we entertained our two Polish aircrew friends Henryk and Wolf for dinner.

After dinner we left the Grand Hotel and thought we would go into the Green Dragon[1] for a drink as we came across the place on our after dinner stroll and none of us had been there before. (It was very rare for me to go into a pub as I hated the smoky atmosphere – although I had been brought up to accept drink as part of life's pleasures from a very early age).

---

[1] In those days the Green Dragon Inn was on the corner of Waterside North and Magpie Square. Demolished in the late 1950's when the 16th C. Merchant's House "The Great Garretes" a little further along the Waterside was restored and became the new Green Dragon. (Lincolnshire Gazette,10th-23rd Nov.2001)

I was in rather a gloomy frame of mind that night, for I had almost completed my five years and eight days as a volunteer in the WAAF but had no idea where my future lay; particularly as my mother was no longer alive. I know that I drank at least one rum, one gin and one vodka (I eschewed whisky and brandy for, as a child living in the country, if toothache occurred the remedy was a piece of cotton wool soaked in one or other of them and placed on the aching tooth. Even now, the smell of whisky or brandy makes me think of toothache!) Anyway, I do know that I placed a glass in the centre of our table and having drunk half or thereabouts of each drink put the remainder in the tumbler in the centre of the table. When we had finished chatting and decided to leave, I picked up the tumbler with its very mixed contents and downed the lot.

It was a clear frosty night with a brilliant full moon when we left the Green Dragon. We went along the side of the River Witham only separated from the moonlit water by a couple of widely spaced wooden rails and we watched a small group of swans peacefully gliding along. Beryl was somewhat squiffy and was determined to go through the rails saying she wanted 'to stroke the swans'. Eventually we made our unsteady way to the High Street and were going along it southwards and that we had to reprimand Beryl for not walking properly.

I do not remember the next bit. I am told that Henryk and Wolf hoped to sober us up by keeping us walking and they got us as far as the seats at the bottom end of the High Street by South Park. Presumably Beryl was feeling a bit more compos mentis by then for she and Wolf left to find a taxi for me, leaving Henryk in charge of me. I am told that a taxi was obtained and the four of us were taken to the Grand Hotel. The Night Porter asked how many were staying and was told just the two girls. I am told that I was carried upstairs by Henryk and Wolf and they put me to bed. Turning over during the night I became aware that I was not alone in the bed. Shocked horror came over me! Who was there in the bed? What would happen if the maid came into the bedroom in the morning and discovered that there had been a man in the bedroom all night? Would news of these shocking goings-on reach my family? I had no idea where the light switch was and the room was in complete darkness because of the blackout. I repeatedly called to Beryl to wake up because "...there is someone in my bed! What shall we do if someone finds him here?" Eventually Beryl woke up and found the light switch. To my tremendous relief I then realised that we were the only two occupants of the room and it was Beryl's feet that I had come across whilst turning over in the double bed we shared.

River Witham, Lincoln 1998 not 1945! Photograph taken by Beryl Commin

Nevertheless I was very puzzled to find that I was still completely dressed with the exception of skirt, jacket and shoes – even my collar and tie were in place – no wonder I felt rather too warm in bed. When it came to going down for breakfast Beryl said she didn't want any. I tried to brazen it out and told her she would feel better if she had some – which she doubted. When we were actually sitting at the breakfast table all I could manage was a cup of tea and some toast."

My leave had started and I was due to stay with my eldest half-sister, Ivy, at the Old Hall at Leadenham for Christmas, so I spent the morning sitting quietly in the NAAFI Club until I felt strong enough to cope with the bouncing of the Lincolnshire Road Car bus for the twelve or so miles to Leadenham. What made things difficult was that somewhere during the previous evening I had lost my WAAF cap – and it has never been found from that day to this. It had my name and number in the brim. I always wonder if it fell off on the staircase of the Grand as I was being carried upstairs by our Polish friends – or did it end up in the taxi cab – or was it left at the Green Dragon?[1] I wish I knew. I do know that I had an anxious time trying to avoid all the "red-caps"[2]. I could not tell them I had lost it but did not know when or how! A likely story! Apart from the risk of being put on a charge for not wearing a cap my main distress at its loss was because I no longer had my beautifully worn nearly smooth cap badge which looked so super after five years of daily polishing and I had planned to take it back with me into Civvy Street as a souvenir to keep of my WAAF life.

Henryk and Wolf were fun to be with, and Wolf was perfectly behaved with us. In fact, Beryl tells me that when she and Wolf went to search for a taxi to get me from South Park to the Grand Hotel, it was Wolf who told Henryk to be on his best behaviour and to guard me carefully.

As a souvenir of Henryk I still have a Polish Cookery Book by Zofja Nowosielska first published by the Polish Library, Glasgow in 1942, revised and enlarged edition November

----

[1] A few years ago I went to the Grand and enquired whether they still have a WAAF cap in their "Lost Property". Sadly, no trace.

[2] Service Police who wore red covers to their caps

1945. Inscribed within is "To Silvia from Henryk with best wishes. Happy Xmas & New Year. 21.XII.45." Recipes include "Nozki Panierowane" (Veal feet in batter) and "Podczos" (Turnip leaves dish). I shamefacedly admit that, although I have had the book for fifty years I still haven't been tempted to try out any of the recipes.

Polish Cookery Book by Zofja Nowosielska

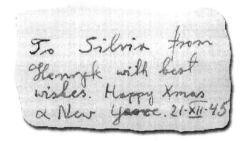

Dedication by Henryk inside cookery book

Extracts from the inside of the book cover read: "During the centuries of their struggle for their existence the Poles have been forced to realise how important is the appropriate nourishment of the body." and "The kitchen is a laboratory of health and happiness. Dishes prepared the Polish way have many advantages; they are nourishing; restorative; diverse and cheap... produce strength and energy for physical and mental work." Here are some examples:

"SZARY BARSZCZ" (Grey Broth)

1 breakfastcupful Pig's Blood	1 small carrot
¼ lb. Heart	
¼ lb. Liver	1 tablespoonful Flour
¼ lb. Lung	Salt
1 small Onion	2 Bay leaves
A small piece of Parsnip	4 pints Water
A small piece Celery	10 Peppercorns

Wash all the meats. Boil for 15 minutes. Take off all scum. Add vegetables and bay leaves. Boil until all are tender. Strain. Cut meats into dices and slice carrot finely. Put into soup. Mix blood well with vinegar and flour until it is creamy; add salt. Boil 6 minutes. Serve with mashed potatoes sprinkled with browned chopped bacon.

STUFFED PIKE

Pike	1 teaspoonful Parsley
1 Egg	A pinch Thyme
1 tablespoonful Breadcrumbs	1 Bay Leaf
1 small Onion	4 Cloves
A pinch Nutmeg	Salt and Pepper

Clean pike. Cut off head. Remove skin completely in one piece. Fillet and mince the fish. Add bread crumbs, grated onion, nutmeg, thyme, parsley, seasoning and egg. Mix well. Use this to loosely stuff the whole skin. Sew up carefully. Roll in cloth. Place in hot water. Add salt, cloves and bay leaf. Simmer slowly for 25 minutes. Serve fish with mayonnaise. Decorate with parsley.

12. *To Bridget – A Son*

In my previous book I told how my mare Bridget spent two years with me when I was posted to R.A.F. Cottesmore in January, 1941. Then I described how I took Bridget with me when I was posted to R.A.F. Coningsby in March, 1943. Not long afterwards a mating for her was arranged with a well-bred Thoroughbred stallion at the village of Frithville not far away.

I also described how, the following Spring, I led a heavily expectant mare to Leadenham to foal. After the first few miles Bridget refused to go faster than walking pace until she espied my sister Ivy and her daughter Joy both riding to meet me as I had desperately telephoned them for assistance. We met near Byard's Leap and from then on, with one of them leading Bridget, our pace increased dramatically and I now had to pedal furiously on my bicycle in order to keep pace with them. Not long after that trek was accomplished I received the good news that Bridget was safely delivered of a son.

Needless to say, as soon as I got a day off, I shot over to Leadenham to see mare and foal. One of my childhood ambitions had been realised – I had bred a foal from my very own mare.

I peeped over the stable door but the new arrival was invisible at first as he was standing behind his mother. I then went into the loose box to see him closely, however, he quickly dodged round the tail or under the neck of Bridget so that I could not touch him. When these ways of avoiding me were thwarted he was able to squeeze beneath Bridget's tummy to get beyond my reach – in other words "he was very small but beautifully formed".

Biddy was an excellent mother and when they were turned out into the orchard it was amusing to see her canter away through the long grass followed by what looked like a large red fox, her son, dashing along behind her – little head and neck stretched out in front of his gingery coloured body and bright bushy fox like tail stuck straight out behind him.

As his mother was "Biddy" and his father "Burgundian" we decided that "Red Wine" would be a suitable name for him – Red[1] for short. As I feared likely, Red inherited the rather hot headed nature of both his parents. However, he was a perfect gentleman in every respect except that he hated any other equine to be in front of him – always wanting to turn a quiet hack out with another horse into a race.

After Red had been weaned I rode Bridget over to be near to me at Morton Hall. Mr Sturgess, who was a large farmer at Eagle Hall (about two miles away), most generously kept Bridget at grass for me free from any charge. I rarely rode her but I remember cycling over to Eagle Hall on several evenings with Tom and being served with the most wonderful meals.

In the summer of 1944 Mr Sturgess's daughter, Peggy, and I decided we would ride over to the north of Lincoln to take part in a Horse Show/Gymkhana to be held in the lovely grounds of Burton Hall. Happily Tom was able to come over from R.A.F. Waddington, as I wanted him to see something

----

[1] Red Biddy (slang) – a cheap red wine with added methylated spirits.

truly English. We all had a lovely afternoon in glorious un-English sunshine.

Eagle Hall is listed as being twelve miles south-west of Lincoln. So it is hardly surprising that riding back along the very long Lincoln High Street at walking pace, followed by a considerable distance along unmarked country lanes was, for me at least, very wearisome and blister-making. I think Bridget was reasonably happy as she had the company of Peggy's pony.

On another occasion I rode Bridget over to stay with my friend June near Saxilby, as I wanted to ride with her at Sturton Show. The following day Biddy was lame. June's mother suggested putting a bandage on the mare's foreleg using embrocation she had successfully used on her husband's back. After twenty-four hours there was no improvement. After a second application when I went to the gate and called her Biddy looked up, waved a foreleg in the air and said she was still poorly. On removing the bandage I was horrified to see lots of little "bubbles" – I had blistered the poor mare. I had no idea – until then – that a lotion which could be put on a bare human back could not be safely used on the hairy leg of a horse!

This made me realise that the time had come for Bridget to be "demobbed". As she had been playing polo when serving with the Royal Ulster Fusiliers this had inevitably caused great strain on her legs – particularly the hind ones due to the sudden braking and acceleration and the twisting and turning demanded from a polo pony in the course of a match. In the winter months when Bridget spent long hours standing in her stable in the garden her hind legs used to become very puffy. This was quite painless for her and the swelling would almost disappear after she had been exercised for an hour or so.

After Biddy left the Army she spent five years with me at R.A.F. Cottesmore, R.A.F. Coningsby and finally at R.A.F. Morton Hall. Her fiery competitive spirit was still as strong as ever but although "the spirit was willing, her legs were weak". I was very happy when my great friend June agreed to give her a home as a brood mare and so ended my beloved mare Bridget's career in the Army and as my companion in the WAAF.

When my demob date had almost arrived I realised that when I went home to Saxilby as a civilian I should have a lot of time on my hands – I did not intend housework to take up much of my time. So what could I find to ride?

I asked around and discovered that on the far side of Swinderby airfield there lived a farmer who had a horse for sale so I cycled over to see them both.

In the summer horses have short glossy coats, however, those which live out of doors in the winter grow much thicker and longer hair which, when plastered with mud through rolling and with a generous coating of natural oils, provides a horse with the equivalent of a Gore-Tex coat for the winter, keeping it relatively warm and waterproof. Therefore, as it was midwinter I was not surprised to be shown a shaggy, rough-looking, bay gelding who looked as if he would be more at home pulling a baker's cart than wearing a saddle and bridle and being ridden.

Nevertheless, as there was no other possible purchase on the horizon I decided to buy "Gay Boy" (as I named him) for the princely sum of £35 – this represented about ten month's pay that I was earning as a WAAF corporal.

Gay Boy was given that name by me because he was a happy, cheerful, good-natured animal and at that time the name 'Gay Boy' had not gained any other meaning than that! Nevertheless, he was usually referred to as "Gutsy" as he had a huge appetite and was always asking for more to eat.

So I rode my new purchase home to Saxilby shortly before my release and looked forward to the time when I could clip off his thick winter coat, put him in Bridget's stable in the back garden with warm rugs on to replace his own "winter woollies" and find out what he really looked like when clipped, his mane, tail and heels trimmed and he had had a proper "beauty treatment" at my hands.

When I was a civilian once again I planned to give myself a treat. I had never had a riding lesson in my life although I had read many books on how to ride correctly. However, unless you are in a large indoor riding school with mirrors around the walls and a good instructor it is really very difficult to know whether or not one is sitting correctly at all paces. I used to ask friends and other riders whether or not they thought my position in the saddle was a good one but got little help from them. Their reply was usually something like "What are you worried about? You don't fall off do you?"

So when I was still a WAAF at Morton Hall I read that the illustrious captain of the famous all-conquering Irish Army Show Jumping Team, Major Jed O'Dwyer, was coming over to England in the Spring of 1946 to take a course at Tony Colling's top-notch Riding School at Porlock in Somerset. Only twelve horses and riders would be accepted for this "one-off" course and they would be the first civilians ever to receive instruction from this famous Irish Team Captain. "Nothing ventured, nothing gained" must have been in my mind as I wrote off for a place on this prestigious course. To my surprised delight I was accepted – perhaps the organisers of the course took pity on a WAAF with an R.A.F. address and little experience applying – as no one queried whether or not I was good enough to meet the demands of the course. I knew that my recently bought "Gay Boy" would certainly not be a suitable mount for me – I didn't think he even knew how to jump anything.

So with young Red at Leadenham, Bridget with June at Ingleby, near Saxilby, and Gay Boy ready to be ridden home to Saxilby I awaited my return to civvy street prepared for some fun ahead.

13. *Demob*

For several months I had been restlessly awaiting the date of my Release from the WAAF and at last it came. It was 8th January, 1946 and I was duly issued with a Return Railway warrant from Swinderby to attend No. 105 Dispersal Centre at Wythall, Birmingham.

I have vague memories of a typically cold and depressing January day with nothing cheery about it at all. Shuttle loads of WAAFs were being taken from the station to the Dispersal Centre and into long wooden wartime service huts where we queued to hand in and account for all our kit with the exception of greatcoats. These could be handed in at a later date at our Unit, Dispersal Centre or Railway Station when 30/- (£1.50) would be given in exchange. I kept mine.

In my R.A.F. Service and Release Book (Form 1250) I see that I was entitled to a Class A Release in Age and Service Group 37. A Class B Release would have meant that I had been released at the request of the Ministry of Labour and National Service and "you will be instructed by that Ministry to your reconstruction work for the purposes to which you have been released". With effect from 3.9.44 my daily pay had gone up from 4/4d per day to 5/- per day. On 12.2.45 it was increased to 5/4d per day.

Presumably we all had some sort of medical exam but I do not remember anything resembling that occurring. Perhaps the fact that we were fit enough to attend the P.D.C. and hand in our kit was proof enough that our fitness was A.1! I did not see anyone I knew and I got the impression that the quicker we were dealt with and left the better.

I was soon on the bus to be taken to the railway station for the return journey to Swinderby, the half mile walk to Morton Hall and then to "get cleared" and pack up one's possessions and depart to civvy street once again. I had handed in all my kit with the exception of what I was wearing, nevertheless, I was surprised to find I had accumulated a considerable amount of odds and ends in the two and a quarter years I had spent at Morton Hall. They just refused to be contained by my kitbag, small suitcase and bomb box. (The last named weighed 16lbs when EMPTY!)

Eventually I managed to get everything to the NAAFI Club near Mint Street, in Lincoln and stowed it all in the foyer, pausing for a break and refreshment before taking my belongings to the Brayford bus stop for the final part of the journey to Saxilby. This inevitably meant that I had to make more than one trip to carry everything. When I returned for my final load I found that one item, very precious to me, had been stolen – a large square biscuit tin containing letters and photos which I treasured. Perhaps someone thought the tin still contained biscuits? The thief would be disappointed. So was I – foolishly trusting as ever – even after five years and eight days as a WAAF. Nevertheless it was really stupid of me to leave it unattended for twenty minutes or so. Also in the tin was a pretty mother of pearl "tikki" which my New Zealand cousin Harold had given me to keep me safe from danger as well as half a silver threepenny bit on a chain from another boyfriend. Luckily my big leather covered zipped writing case (a legacy from Boarding School days in Ambleside) had been packed elsewhere as it contained a number of photographs which I have used in these two books.

It only took Hutson's bus about twenty minutes to drop me at the front gate of my home at Saxilby (no "official" bus stops in those days).

Five years earlier I had left "White Lodge" full of pleasurable excitement because I could at last become a WAAF. Strangely, although I had been restlessly awaiting my demob for several months, now that it had actually occurred I cannot recall any "pleasurable excitement" on returning home to resume civilian life once again.

Perhaps it was because the world was now a very different place and I was now a very different person with very different feelings. In other words – I had grown up.

OLD BOMBER BASE REVISITED
A Pilot's Pilgrimage to the past

by **Jim McCorkle**, ex-R.A.F. pilot[1]

Deserted, abandoned, an airfield spans the lonely heath.
Unkempt broken runways sprout their share of grass and weeds.
Bare dispersal pans of circular concrete sit, now empty.
Lacking the black silhouettes of the bombers,
Which used to squat, etched against the darkening sky.

Empty pre-fab huts, with broken glassless windows,
Gaze sightlessly out at overgrown hedgerows,
And seem to echo back the voices and laughter of youths,
Who, in blue, once rode the skies to destruction and death.

----

[1] The holder of the copyright of this poem is invited to contact the author of this book.

The wind sighs in lonely desolation as if recalling
The vibrant roar of countless Merlins, coughing
Puffs of blue smoke to be whirled away
In the swirling propwash of many Lancs,
Ponderously thundering into the clouds and, when massing,
Made the very Earth tremble with their passing.
Where groundcrew kept tally of every departure,
And muttered a prayer for each aerial charger;
Throughout the long nights their vigils maintained,
'Til in the grey dawn, their visages strained,
They counted the losses.

A strange life, to protect a way of living!
Sacrifice demanded, and the ultimate too often given.

A lonely figure walked to where a runway ended.
Thoughts deep in the past as his spirit blended.
Seeing this airfield as he once knew it.
Remembering well! He'd flown, and lived through it.

Exorcising ghosts, he roamed o'er the acres,
Recalling faces, nicknames of givers and takers.
Pilots, Navs, and Flight Engineers too,
Wireless Ops, Gunners, from each motley crew.

But the visions all vanished. The noises dimmed.
'Til all that remained was the sigh of the wind:
A creaking window, the rustle of grass.
Returned to the present. Bid Adieu to the past.

(Royal Air Force 1995)

14. *Fifty Years On – Ken*

Just before Ken returned to Oz we had a farewell dinner together at the Albion Hotel.

Ken naturally thought my plans to marry Jimmy were going ahead as I hadn't dared raise Ken's hopes by telling him that Jimmy and I had split up.

Here are some extracts from Ken's post-war letters to me at my home in Saxilby, six miles north-west of Lincoln.

25th July, 1946

My Dear Sylvia,

It is ever so strange to think that I was wondering whether you would be married ere this, as last time we dined together you acted rather well, as I wasn't the least suspicious of anything amiss between you and Jimmy.

Well anyway pal, let us forget about that, but I am awfully sorry to hear the unfortunate news. Glad that I had given you my home address, as I guess it may have been some time before I wrote to you, then I would have feared causing trouble between Jimmy and you......

Happy to say I have been demobbed 1st April and started work on the 8th and haven't missed a day since. I even did a month during my 40 days leave on arriving back in Aussie.

I was in a hurry to bank money for I won £400 on the trip and was glad to get rid of the roll of notes I had been carrying around for so long. We arrived in Melbourne on the 3rd January and both Mum and Dad were both down to meet the ship. We were given leave straight from the ship, and after having 10 days leave visit-

ing friends with Mum I was glad to get back to good old Mildura and start work. I hardly know a soul but went to every dance to make up for lost time.

After leave I went back to be demobbed and insisted on having that operation on my nose done and then got demobbed on 1st April. Lorne you asked after, was married just before I arrived home and has since become a mother of a son. I haven't seen Beattie, she cleared out with a married man the day I arrived in port. So you are not to be left out being a spinster, I look like being a bachelor.

Glad to hear you are taking a bit of time out between horse shows to do some housework. It will be to your advantage in later years my girl.........I intend to be a bookmaker one of these days. I have started on a small scale and have been clearing £6-£10 every week.

Have just bought mother a house and intend to build myself one as soon as things get plentiful as I have bought the land. I am working back at the shed not as a storeman but as citrus clerk, less work and better pay. They gave me £100 bonus on returning and I got another yearly bonus today £12, so you see I am saving money. Goodness knows what I shall do with it all, may even have a trip to Blighty again before I die. Might even go to the extent of getting you to come out and be a spinster along side of me. You could have a string of racehorses. What could be better than that.

Gosh what a cheap holiday £50. I have been anticipating a trip to New Zealand in the next 2-3 years. I estimate that shall cost me about £500, but I hope to win that in a few months when I get settled down to bookmaking and I shall have to spend it somehow.

So you heard from Tom. I guess he would be rather anxious to have his bride out here. All of my friends are out of the Forces and back at work. One is married, another engaged...... Reg and myself haven't any prospects. I can see I slipped badly not getting me an English bride. Would you consider having me back as a boy friend, Sylvia, and see if we can make things plan. No, I thought as much. I can't blame you. I have been going to the dances twice a week and playing football every weekend so I get very little time to myself, the least the better I find as it gives me very little time to think.

I'm in first class health myself, and it all seems like a dream but gosh the memories. I haven't got any of your letters to peruse over, as I burnt them all when I left Binbrook as I didn't think there would be any need for them. Gosh, Sylvia, you have been a great pal to me as you always seem to turn up at the right time to give me a little bit extra encouragement. I think it may have turned out a bit better had I been a little more passionate. What do you think? I know, don't tell me, we are just good pals. I bet Les would be awful glad to see you again. Yes, we would have a terrible lot to talk about if we ever got near each other. I would be looking for that Gretna Green I never got around to when we visited Edinburgh.

Just imagine 2 yrs ago tonight I went to Stuttgart. Gosh the time has flown. So Anne got married. When you write to your Aunt give her my regards and ask her how her garden grows.

Well, my dear, I am just the same as ever and could go on writing page after page to you once I start, but it is only boring to you old pal, but see hear and be sure that you write so I shall be anxious to hear from you.........

So in the meantime keep the old chin up as there's always a silver lining somewhere. Sorry I haven't got a spare parrot to oblige you. Give Red Wine a pat from me, and maybe have dinner at the Albion one of these nights, just for old time's sake. Cheerio, Sylvia, pal and all the best till next time. I hope it will not be as long as the last time and you've got yourself a penfriend for life, I swear.

Yours as ever,
Devoted Pal,
Ken

To Bosworth House, Huntingdon, 30th November, 1947:

My Dear Sylvia,

I was ever so glad to receive your very welcome letter the other day......... I don't say we will have a wizard time (this Christmas) just a little bit out of the ordinary but far below the par of pre war but I guess a bit better than you less fortunate people over there. I often wonder what we fought the war for as for a victorious side, I think England are worse off than Germany. .... No Sylvia, I had a far better time in England than I have ever had the pleasure to spend here at home.

It does not sound like the Sylvia I knew to be getting discouraged like that and saying you will be a real old woman by the time you marry. What of me, may I ask, for I have not even got any prospects – I am not anxious as I am quite satisfied that I am not the marrying kind. Do you know I've not even been out with a girl since last Boxing Night.

Yes, Sylvia, I have got a good job and like it quite well. No, I have not given up the idea of accountancy, and will do it in due course. I have had a promotion in my job since I last wrote and I am in line for a better job in the days to come, so I shall be quite contented to stay with this firm.

Well, Sylvia, I do not do very much except play football during the winter and cricket during the summer. Usually of a Sunday I garden in the morning then go swimming all the afternoon. I usually go dancing Wed. and Sat. nights. I am beginning to get too old to dance so I am contemplating advertising through some matrimonial agency to find a widow looking for a husband; I am quite convinced that is the only way I'll get a wife. I'm afraid you will not believe it when I tell you I am too shy. I met quite a few of my old Air Force companions on a recent three week holiday to Melbourne and it was good to recollect old times. I would give anything to be able to turn the clock back to England again, still I had my chance and I never grasped it[1].........

Do not forget to keep the chin up and smile, just for Ken, Sylvia.

Do you know your photo is the pride of place on my dressing table. I will send you a photo of me in civvies one day soon.[2]

Yours as ever,

Ken

Letter to The Rookery, Fenstanton, Huntingdon dated 20th February, 1948:

Dear Sylvia.

"I was apparently dozing when Mum brought the letters in and put them on the dressing table and the moment I saw them I felt better as I had just about given you up for desertion, but under the circumstances you are exonerated entirely."

"Poor Sylvia, you have certainly had your share of outs the past 2 years, it is now time that you and Leslie had better luck."

"Did I tell you the house we were living in was sold and we had to get out. My people weren't in a position to buy a place so I bought one for them, that is the present address you will note..."

"In November that year 2 of my football mates accompanied me to Adelaide for holiday, 3 wks in all, had a grand time, done the Gulf trip. It was rather an expensive trip though for 3 wks cost me £200, lost about £170 on the horses as I had probably told you I was doing a bit of book-making. I had won it so easy come easy go. I just could not strike it lucky at all, it taught me a lesson, though a pretty expensive lesson you will agree. I soon made it up during the year and in March '47 we were fortunate to move into our own home, it has only been up 9 years and quite modern to the house we were living in before, although badly in need of a

---

[1] Ken had been offered a job at Aussie H.Q. in London but turned it down as he would have had to wear civilian clothes and not worn his uniform.

[2] This was never received.

coat of paint both inside and out. So while Mum went away for 6 weeks holiday Dad and I got down to business in earnest, done the inside and out you should have seen the mess we had, it would have broken any woman's heart to see it but we had it spotless by the time mum returned and she was quite pleased with the effort."

"By this time we had a fair garden under cultivation also and that used to keep me busy in all my leisure hours either weeding or mowing the lawn. Then I took on the job of painting it outside. Gosh I never thought I would ever complete it, took me about 5 weekends, but it was worth it as it looks all the better for it. I painted it cream and green after it had been brick and chocolate color. I get quite a kick out of it now when people going past comment on how different the place looks. I almost burst the buttons off my shirt with pride."

"I spend all my leisure time around the house doing odd jobs that I have not done any more to my accountancy course that I started 18 months[1] ago since we shifted to the new house. I don't think I shall have any call to use it in my present job which will do me until I leave it to take on bookmaking seriously."

"In November my 2 pals and myself went to Tasmania for a fortnight's holiday, a week in Launceston and a week in Hobart. Gosh, it's a wizard place for all the world like England green and picturesque and the people are very hospitable."

..."I am now planning to go to N.Z. for next vacation. I am looking for a companion but the majority of the working lads can't afford to go over there as it would cost between £150 and £200 to have a really worthwhile trip over there. One would have to have 6 weeks off as it is 5 days by boat from Sydney and if one spent so much to go there they may as well see the lot as half of it (this will be the honeymoon that I have always hoped for but will

---

[1] Ken was happy working with figures – as his bookmaking hobby proved. Therefore, I encouraged him to take up accountancy so that he could obtain a job which would use his undoubted abilities and be more satisfying than that of fruit grader.

be alone Sylvia). This will sound hard to believe, Sylvia, but I just don't have any time for the fairer sex these days. I intend to be a bachelor. Doesn't sound like me talking. When you used to talk about your cat and bird and being an Old Maid, I used to scorn at you. Now the boot is on the other foot."

"It's funny I was only thinking of you the other week when a show "Weekend at the Waldorf" appeared here for the first time. Do you remember us going to it in London that time you were down when I was working at Headquarters? That must be 3 yrs ago almost anyway."

"Gosh time flies these days. I have just lost track of it and just contented with 3 feeds a day and a bed apart from a little bit of work between meals there is little else to worry me".

"I hope you will forgive my terrible scrawl, not that I could improve my English if I live to be a hundred, you will know that too well, better than me in fact."

"Regards to the folk at Leadenham also Uncle and Aunt at Gosport not forgetting Leslie of course. Cheerio for the present pal and all the best that is good for you Sylvia."

Affectionately Yours,

As Ever, Ken

Air Letters from Ken 105 San Mateo Ave, Mildura, Victoria, Australia to Miss Sylvia Pickering, The Old Hall, Leadenham, Lincoln, England. Date: 4th April, 1948

Dear Sylvia,

I guess it is high time I got to write you a note my friend, as I have been rather neglectful on the pen of late, apparently over-done it in the Services and intend to do as little as possible now. Yes, I am quite well again. That bout wasn't anything very bad just a severe inflamed throat really, but the doctors have some fancy name for it I can not even pronounce it let alone write it, still as ignorant and as crude as ever you will agree.

Well Sylvia, I hope everything is still going O.K. with you and Leslie. I am still the confirmed bachelor, likely to be for some time yet. Two of my pals got themselves engaged at Easter, one is to be married on 19th June, I'm to be best man!

We are very busy at the shed right now, right in the swing with the fruit. I have got a good easy job, fruit classer at the door. That is classing the fruit into grades as it comes into the shed, good money and no manual labour.

I have just knocked off from duties in the garden for a while to pen you this note, as we are getting into Autumn I must get the vegetables blooming before the winter sets in. I must also get to work to paint the house, as I have just completed painting the roof.

By the way, I bought a motor cycle and side car the day after I wrote to you and its very handy to ride backwards and forwards to work, also for football. Yes, we are well in training for football. My foot went on me in the first practice game about a fortnight ago and I have been resting it well. Tried it out yesterday and it seems O.K. again.

Yes, the op on the nose was very successful except I got a bump on it at football training the other night and boy did it tingle.

I hope you were successful in getting your secretarial post. Hope everyone at Leadenham is well. Pass on my best wishes also a handful of oats to "Red Wine" in preference to a kiss, you can have that my angel.

I should imagine that Anne has settled right down now, especially with a family to keep her busy.

How did you go in your point to point races? I suppose a couple of wins and a couple of places as usual. You're too good lady, you should give the others a chance.

Well Sylvia, old pal, space is limited and I will have to leave you for the time being.

Please excuse the mistakes both in writing and grammar. I'm afraid that I will never learn.

Cheerio till next time my old pal.

Your old cobber, Ken

The last time I had contact with Ken was from his letter to me of 4th April, 1948. I subsequently wrote to him at his usual address but had no reply, nor was my letter returned to me.

In 1995 I asked Ted Richardson if he could find out whether or not my old Aussie friend was still alive. Ted gave me the sad news that Ken had died on 18th March, 1989 and he also gave me the name of 460 R.A.A.F. Squadron Secretary in Australia to see if anyone could be found who remembered him. Here are excerpts from Robby Robson's letter to me of 10th May, 1995:

> *"Dear Sylvia,*
>
> *I am sorry you received the sad news of Ken's passing through the Veterans' Affairs Office......... I have found Ken in the Squadron Operations records. As I thought he was on the Squadron July to September 1944. He did Stuttgart on 28th/29th July, so he was a week or two out in his recollection of this operation. All his other trips were over France – the following is his crew:*
>
> | | |
> |---|---|
> | *Pilot:* | *F/O Murray, J. K.* |
> | *F/Eng:* | *Sgt. Phipps, H. G. (probably R.A.F.)* |
> | *Bomb Aimer:* | *F/Sgt. Colsby, J.A.* |
> | *Navigator:* | *Sgt. Manley, F. (Could also have been R.A.F.)* |
> | *W/Op:* | *F/Sgt. Chapman, V.* |
> | *M/U A/G:* | *F/Sgt. K. ....* |
> | *Rear A/G:* | *F/Sgt. Low, R. T.* |
>
> *Unfortunately none of his crew are active in our Association. None of the names are familiar to me........."*

Ted Richardson said he liked several of the little stories I had started to write about my time in the WAAF and suggested I write to Norman Small in Oz who was collecting stories from ex-WAAF to publish in a book in memory of his wife, Elizabeth, who had recently died. By the time I did this Norman's wonderful collection of stories entitled "Spit, Polish and Tears" had been sent to the publishers so nothing of mine was included in it.

I told Norman, who had also served in 460 RAAF Squadron, about my friendship with Ken, and that I had had no reply to my subsequent letters and Norman generously offered to see if he could trace any of Ken's relations and, after only four telephone calls, managed to contact Ken's older sister, Edie. This is the letter I received from Edie, probably Christmas 1997:

"Dear Sylvia,

Sorry I have taken so long to write to you but I am not a letter writer, but if I can help you I will. Ken was my brother, five years younger than I, he was very special to me, I loved him dearly. The war took its toll on him. He had a heart condition for quite a while, almost died a few times – died in March '89. He always loved to dance and died on the dance floor.[1]

He married Margaret in '62, they had 12 years courtship. Margaret was 38 when they married. She also loved to dance, and has now started to dance again. A lovely girl. We ring each other every week and so keep in touch a lot.

Son Wayne died suddenly[2], left little Harley aged 5, and a little girl aged 2. They are the light of Margaret's life, and Mark the other son is a plumber and has a good business. He is not married but has a nice girl friend.

Ken had a "Crown & Anchor" board and made a lot of money on the way home, so bought a home for mum and Dad to live in. He was so good to them.........

----

[1] He had just passed Margaret – smiled at her and collapsed (information from Norman Small)

[2] Early in 1995

> *He moved to Melbourne to marry Marg, got a transfer in his job, because she lived with her mother – lost her father when she was 10 years old – an only child. So good to her Mother and good to our parents also.........*
>
> *I had my 80th birthday last year but keep fit. Walk every morning and swim twice a week in a heated pool. Have been swimming 18 years. Now my dear if I can help you any way Norm Small said you would like to know a few details of what happened to Ken.*
>
> *With kind regards,*
> *Edie*
>
> *P.S. I have 2 grandchildren – boy Ian 25 and girl Lisa. Have just come back from Scotland and Ireland Had a lovely time."*

In a Christmas card from Edie she told me that she had –

> *"just had Ken's wife, Margaret, to stay for a couple of weeks. Margaret had been engaged before but my Mother was very possessive of Ken and she and Ken lived together and would not go and meet Mum. I had met her, of course, and she did live in Melbourne. Ken did very well when he went to Melbourne. He did a type of accountancy and was a Collecting Clerk for a large firm and was well looked after, also did bookmaking.*
>
> *I think the stress of the Air Force so young was one of the causes of his death. Ken was a wonderful father and they lived with Margaret's Mother, who was a lovely lady and was good to them. This will answer some of your questions.*
>
> *Kind regards, Edie."*

(The Christmas card read: *To Sylvia wishing you Health and Happiness for Xmas and in 1998*).

I am fascinated that Margaret and Ken had a twelve year engagement. I can understand that Ken's Mother would not wish to lose the support of Ken if he married and moved to Melbourne. What I cannot understand is that Margaret would never go to meet Ken's mother. I wonder if they ever met or did the wedding take place only after the death of Ken's Mother? I am intrigued. What would have happened if I had married Ken in England and I had turned up as a "war bride"? I wonder what sort of reception I should have had! I am quite sure that Ken found the right wife for him at last, as Margaret looks really lovely, with a kind and gentle nature and I am sure they were blissfully happy together.

Margaret and Ken, March, 1989

15. *Fifty Years On – Tom*

Shortly after returning home to Saxilby after being demobbed I had a lovely surprise. It came in the shape of a well worn rather scruffy airmail letter postmarked Sydney, Australia and was dated 4th January, 1946. The sender was Flying Officer T. P. Whiteley, RAAf, Bradfield Park, New South Wales, Australia and was addressed to:-

Miss Sylvia Pickering,
White Lodge,
.................,
Lincolnshire,
England.
(Late Cpl. Pickering, H.Q. 5 Group, Swinderby, Lincoln).

It was re-addressed to me with a sticker on it which read "R.A.F. Postal Service." "Reason for re-direction – Release"

My Dear Sylvia,
Just a few lines to wish you a Happy New Year, although it will be rather late by the time it reaches you. So sorry that I missed such a grand pal as you for Xmas.

Really dear, I could not think of your address. Hope its right now.

I am still in the Service and I suppose you are also.

How is the horse riding going old pal? Still taking all the prizes.

> *So far my wife is not out here. But hoping she will be on her way soon. By the way have you still got that little snap I sent you of her. If so, old girl, I'd love to have it back.*
>
> *I suppose you are married now. If so I do hope the chap is good enough for you. Still I doubt if he would be O.K. in my eyes for you.*
>
> *Tons of love,*
> *Tom X X X X*

I never received the photo, or the letter which probably accompanied it, and I have always wondered what Tom's shy bride looked like. I don't even remember noticing that he was another of my aircrew friends who had been commissioned and that he now held the rank of Flying Officer. When we first met he had been a Sergeant – I wonder when he gained his Commission? But as he was now a married man I did not trust myself to reply to his letter.

Fifty years on I discovered there was a 467/463 RAAF Squadron Association which met at Waddington conveniently close to Lincoln for me to attend and, because of my friendship with Tom, I was allowed to become an Hon. Member. Ted Richardson was then the U.K. Hon. Sec./Treasurer and he has helped me enormously with my research. He had been a navigator with 467 Squadron. Ted gave me details of what happened to Tom and the crew after they had been shot down by night fighters when they were returning from a raid on Bremen on the night of 5th October, 1944, including the report by Sgt. McLellan on his escape when he evaded capture and what happened to him afterwards, as well as copies of the reports of the raids taken from the Operational Record Book at the time. I have put extracts from these reports in Chapter 6 "Tom – Joins 463 RAAF Squadron".

F/O	D. G. Tointon	Pilot	Killed
F/Sgt	R. Broad	Wireless Operator	Killed
F/Sgt	J. MacPherson	Mid Upper Gunner	Killed
F/Sgt	D. E. Brown	Navigator	P.O.W.[1]
F/Sgt	A. Giloran	Bomb Aimer	P.O.W.
F/Sgt	T. Whiteley	Rear Gunner	P.O.W.
Sgt.	J. P. McLellan	Flight Engineer	Evaded capture

Sgt. John Peter W. McLellan was born on 26th November 1922, so was not quite twenty years of age when he joined the Royal Air Force on 28th May, 1942. In civilian life he was an Articled Surveyor who lived at St. Asaph, Flintshire, North Wales. The following is his Official Report:

"I was an Engineer in a Lancaster aircraft returning from a bombing raid on Bremen on the night of 6 Oct. 44 and was shot down by a fighter. I baled out and landed in a pond west of Bremen and near Papenburg, near the Dutch/German frontier. I buried my chute and flying kit and walked for about 1½ hours and then rested in a haystack. I walked in a westerly direction and got to the river Ems which I swam and then proceeded across a field. I saw a man with a horse and cart on the road and thought it best to take no notice, but he caught up with me and spoke in English. I found out that he was a German who had been in America for some years and he gave me a lift to near the border. I waited in a wood until it was dark and crossed over the frontier near Bourtange, and went to the first farmhouse I saw. The people were friendly and I made them understand that I would like to stay the night. They gave me food and lodging and next afternoon a woman came and gave me to understand that I was to remain there until I had other news.

I stayed for three days and then received a note which said "unorganised travelling is dangerous." It also told me that a man

----

[1] Prisoner of War

was to come to the house and I was to cycle 10 metres behind him and we would meet a second man. This one was to meet a third who would shake hands and I was to follow this last man. I carried out these instructions and was taken to a house in Vriescheloo.

The owner of the house was the local parson and head of the underground movement. I stayed for two months until 9th December, 1944. In late October whilst I was at this house, I was told that an American pilot was coming to the house. He arrived and I was surprised to see him greet the parson with a click of the heels and a stiff bow. This made me suspicious of him and especially when I heard him speak. His English was very guttural and his name was Heny Meister. He stayed for about three weeks and my suspicions of him were further aroused by the answers he gave to my questions about the Fortress he was supposed to have flown. I saw him give a letter to the parson's maid and I got hold of this and gave it to the parson. It was addressed to his wife at an address near Berlin. The local Underground were not satisfied with him and he was taken to Gronigen for interrogation. I was later told he had been shot down.

On December 8th, 1944 the Germans searched the house but I was not found as I was hiding between the walls. They took the parson to Gronigen for questioning. That night I left the house and went to Wedde to the house of a land worker I had met at the parson's house. I stayed there for one week. The land worker then found me a place to stay at Ter Wupping north Onstwedde. I stayed at this house until I was liberated in Apr 45 and during this time I helped to clean arms that had been dropped by the R.A.F."

Report map of Sgt. John Peter McLellan after being shot down follow-ing a raid on Bremen. (Not to scale. Map by Jenny Toyne.)

If the world was a fair place, after the war Sgt McLellan would have had a long and happy life to make up for all the wartime stress and strain. It was not to be. Mr. McLellan, who was a very keen footballer and cricketer, worked after the war for B.I.C.C. (British Insulated Calender Cables) and, whilst work-ing on a pylon had a fall and was very badly injured and died about two years afterwards.

F/O Tointon and crew were not the only victims of Ger-man fighter aircraft. On 21st February 1945 Wing

Commander Bill Forbes, D.S.O., D.F.C., who was their Squadron Commander from 25th June, 1944 was also shot down. W/Cdr Forbes, his Wireless Operator and Mid Upper Gunner were killed. The German night fighter pilot who shot them down, shot down seven Lancs in 18 minutes that night, three of them from 463 Squadron.

In June, 1999 I was so pleased to discover that there was an Air Gunners' Association based at RAF Elvington, near York so I immediately wrote off to Mr Fred Stead, chairman of the association to see if there was anything on record about Ken, Jimmy or Tom – the three wartime air gunners who were such close friends of mine. I had the following reply and to my amazement I found he knew of Tom.

26th November, 1999

Dear Sylvia,

I owe you a most sincere apology for not responding to your letter of the 30th. June. Whilst it is not a good excuse I have to admit that my duties on behalf of the Air Gunners' Association, which has a worldwide membership of almost 2000 ex Air gunners, have kept me extremely busy with a continuous stream of correspondence. Most of it involves enquiries like yours which have to be researched and responded to.

Judging by Tom's POW number he would not arrive at Stalag Luft 7, Bankau until well into the second half of 1944. It was a new camp in early June 1944 and my number was 98, after which it began to grow in numbers quite quickly. I think by the time we left in January 1945 there were around 1500 prisoners. I am afraid I cannot claim to have known Tom personally as I spent much of my time working as an orderly in our camp hospital. POWs were a very resourceful lot and numerous activities soon developed with equipment supplied by the Red Cross and YMCA. We had a theatre group, of which I was a member and took part in plays and the Christmas pantomime. There were also a number of study groups and sporting activities.

Of course, all this was left behind when we were obliged to leave in face of the advancing Russian Army. I enclose a copy of the official report submitted to the Protecting Power in Switzerland which will give you some idea of the conditions under which we marched, mostly in temperatures well below zero. Also enclosed are some impressions of the march and the 'sick quarters' on our arrival at Stalag 3, Luchenwalde, drawn by a POW. We had hundreds of men suffering with dysentery and frost bite with little or no medication for them.

Whilst I have no personal experience of publication I am told that this can be an expensive venture. I think you would be well advised to seek advice from someone more knowledgeable than myself in this field. In the meantime we shall retain them in our archives.

Yours sincerely,

Fred Stead

Cartoon by POW.

139

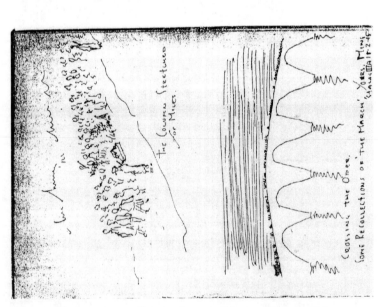

Cartoons by POWs

For the attention of the Swiss Commission, acting as Protecting Power.

REPORT OF A FORCED MARCH MADE BY OCCUPANTS OF STALAG LUFT 7, GERMANY

On January 17th, 1945, at approximately 11 am we received notice of one hour in which to pack our kit and be ready to leave the Camp by marching. At the same time we were informed by Ober Feldwebel Frank that for every one man who fell out of the column on the march, five men would be shot. This order was never given in writing.

The start was postponed until 3.30 am on January 19th. During the interval 68 sick men were evacuated to the civilian Ilag at Kreuzberg. We believe they were later taken to Stalag 344, at Lamsdorf.

Each man was issued with two-and-a-half days marching rations before leaving. When the march began at 3.30 on January 19th, no transport was supplied for any sick who might have fallen out on the march and the only medical equipment carried was that carried by the Medical Officer and three Sanitators on their backs.

Details of march

January 19th: Left Bankau and marched to Winterveldt, a distance of 28 kms. This was done under extremely trying weather conditions and severe cold. The only accommodation at Winterveldt was small barns.

January 20th: Marched from Wintersveldt to Karlsruhe arriving at 10 am. We set off at 5 am and marched a distance of 12 kms. At Karlsruhe we were housed in an abandoned brick factory. Here for the first time we were provided with two field kitchens with which to cook for 1550 men. Each field kitchen was actually capable of cooking sufficient food for 200 men. The Medical Officer was also provided with a horse and cart for the transport of the sick. The cart was big enough to hold 6 sitting cases. Coffee was

141

provided and after a rest period of 11 hours we were again or-dered to move. The Camp Leader and the Medical Officer protested against further marching until the men were ade-quately fed and rested. We were told by the German Abwehr Officer that it was an order and must be complied with. The same night we left Karlsruhe and marched to Schönfeld, arriving at 9 am on January 21st, covering a distance of 42 kms. The condi-tions during the night were extreme, the temperature being –13 degrees Centigrade. The Medical Officer's wagon was filled after the first five kilometres and from onwards, men were being picked up at the roadsides in a collapsed and frozen state and it was only by sheer will-power that they were able to finish the march. After crossing the river Oder, a distance of 34 kms., we were told that we would be accommodated and that no move would be made for two days.

<u>January 21st</u>: At Schönfeld we were accommodated in the cow-sheds and barns of a farm. A room was provided for the sick at Lossen. Rations issued were about 100gms. of biscuits per man and half a cup of coffee.

<u>January 22nd</u>: At 3 am orders were given by the Germans to pre-pare to march off at once. It was dark and there was some delay in getting the men out from their sleeping quarters because they could not find their baggage. The German guards thereupon marched into the quarters and discharged their firearms. The column was marching again by 5 am. Twenty-three men, it was ascertained at this stage, were lost and their whereabouts are un-known. Also, thirty-one men were evacuated (we believe) to Lamsdorf, but nothing further has been heard of them We marched to Jenkwitz, a distance of 34 kms. And were housed at a farm in barns. Here we were issued with a total of 114 kgs. of fat, 46 tins of meat, barley, peas and threequarters of a pig. Soup was issued, the ration being about a quarter of a litre per man. No bread was issued.

<u>January 23rd</u>: Left Jenkwitz at 6 am and marched 20 kms. To Wanzen.

January 24th: We were rested that day at Wanzen, sleeping in barns. The revier was in a cowshed. 31 sick were evacuated to Sagan. 400 loaves of bread were issued.

January 25th: Left Wanzen at 4 a.m. for Keidersdorf. Covered 30 kms.

January 26th: Spent the day at Keidersdorf. Issued with 600 loaves of bread to last for two days.

January 27th: Left Keidersdorf and marched 19 kms. To Pfaffendorf, where we arrived at night.

January 28th: Left Pfaffendorf for Standorf at 5 a.m. and marched a distance of 21 kms. Issued with 24 cartons of knackerbrot, 150 kgs. margarine and 50 kgs. sugar. 22 sick were evacuated to Scheidnitz and eventually arrived at Sagan.

January 29th: Left Standorf at 6 p.m. and marched to Peterwitz a distance of 22 kms. We arrived at 4 a.m. the following day. This march was carried out in darkness under extreme conditions, with a blizzard blowing the whole time. The men arrived at Peterwitz in an utterly exhausted condition. Before leaving Standorf we were promised that we have to march no further as transport would be supplied from Peterwitz. 104 kgs. of meat were issued, 1 sack of salt, 25 kgs. of coffee and l00 kgs. of barley.

January 30th: At Peterwitz 30 men from Stalag 344, who had been left without guards, joined our column. 296 loaves of bread were issued, 50 kgs. oats, and 35.5 kgs. of margarine.

January 31st: We spent the day at Peterwitz. We were told that we would have to march to Goldberg before we got transport. 300 kgs. of oats were issued, 50 kgs. of coffee and 40 kgs. of margarine.

February 1st: We marched from Peterwitz to Prausnitz, a distance of 12 kms. We remained at Prausnitz from February 1st – 5th. On February 1st we were issued with 680 loaves of bread and 37.5 kgs. of margarine. On February 3rd we were issued with 112.5 kgs. of margarine, 250 loaves, 100 kgs. sugar, 200 kgs. flour *and 150 kgs. barley. On February 4th the issue was 150 loaves. At night on February 4th the Commandant (Oberst Leutnant Behr) visited the farm and read out an order from OKW to the effect that five men were to be released and would be liberated at the first opportunity. The purpose of this we were unable to understand*

<u>*February 5th*</u>: *Before leaving we were issued with 500 loaves of bread, 95 kgs. of margarine and 530 tins of meat. We were marched from Prausnitz to Goldberg, a distance of 8 kms. On arrival at Goldberg we were put into cattle trucks, an average of 55 men to each truck. By this time there were numerous cases of dysentery and facilities for men to attend to personal hygiene were inadequate. The majority had no water on the train journey for two days. When the men were allowed out of the trucks to relieve themselves, numerous guards ordered them back inside again and we had to be continually getting permission for the men to be allowed out. We were on the train from the morning of February 5th until the morning of February 8th. Before commencing this journey, we were issued with sufficient rations for two days. The total distance marched was 240 kms.*

SUMMARY

As a result of this march and the deplorable conditions, the morale of the men is extremely low. They are suffering from an extreme degree of malnutrition, and at present, an outbreak of dysentery. There are numerous cases of frost bite and other minor ailments. They are quite unfit for any further movement. Food and better conditions are urgently required. We left Bankau with no Red Cross supplies and throughout the march all the rations were short issued, the most outstanding being bread, which amounts to 2,924 loaves.

....

D. C. Howatson, R.A.M.C.,
Camp Medical Officer
February 15th, 1945.

Route of Tom's forced march of 240km from Bankau to Goldberg (not to scale. Map by Jenny Toyne).

At the Remembrance Day meeting of 467/463 RAAF Squadron in 1997 Ted Richardson told us about the National Arboretum Appeal and I wrote to Mr David Childs, the Director, asking several questions. I particularly wanted to know what details would be kept of the people in whose remembrance the trees were to be planted. I wrote "understandably a plaque will only give brief details of the person or crew represented. I think that what is needed is some 'flesh on the bones' to bring these men back to life again as real people so that those who walk beside the trees in a hundred years time – or more – can feel that the trees represent real people with red blood in their veins and are not just names which say so little in themselves. Try to make each tree alive with as many details as possible so that despite the passage of time the men themselves live on as people – as much alive as the trees planted in memory of them".

In his reply of 17th November, 1997 Mr Childs wrote:

"Thank you for your most thoughtful and helpful letter....... Details such as those you propose would make a most fitting addition if they were placed in another book which could be kept in the Visitor Centre as part of the Reference Library...... I feel most strongly that the spirit of the Arboretum is such that it must endeavour to keep more than just names and basic details alive. We need to clothe them with sufficient detail to create personality in much the same way as the bare branches will get clothed with leaves. The way that you suggest would seem to be the obvious solution".

I subsequently sent a cheque and a dedication together with four stories which I had written about Tom.

"The first two are not stories of great daring in the sky but are still strong memories of two evenings we enjoyed in each other's company... Please let me know if you think the Folder could be usefully kept in the proposed Visitor Centre. There is one thing of which I am quite sure – it is unlikely that you will be asked by anyone else to keep such a story as 'Tom- - and the Bike Ride' as a memorial".

In his reply of 17th December, 1997 Mr Childs wrote:

"Thank you for the four tales of Tom. He must have been a great chap and you obviously had a very special friendship. I will be delighted to keep hold of these and place them in our small Reference Section once the Visitor Centre and Chapel are built. One of the aims of The Arboretum is to keep alive a personality as well as a name; these stories will do just that and I am so pleased to have been given them. They do give an insight into war time Ser-

vice life that is not often seen in the books about the period. That having been said I can recall several fairly similar bike rides in my Service Career!"

A tree has been donated by
ex-WAAF Cpl. PICKERING, J. S.
late of H.Q. 5 GROUP (BOMBER COMMAND)
in memory of the happy times spent together with
FLIGHT SERGEANT TOM P. WHITELEY
who was the REAR GUNNER
In the crew of FLYING OFFICER D. G. TOINTON
They were members of
463 Royal Australian Air Force Lancaster Bomber Squadron
who were stationed at R.A.F. WADDINGTON, LINCOLN
Their aircraft was shot down by GERMAN FIGHTERS
on the night of 5th OCTOBER, 1944
during a raid on BREMEN

Three of the crew were killed;
Three were made Prisoners and one evaded capture.

I have no news of what happened to Tom after he was de-mobbed and began life with his Irish bride. Very many years later I wrote to the address of his parents at Bexley near Sydney for news of him but, not surprisingly, heard nothing nor was my letter returned to me. I had asked the current occupier of the house to kindly forward it to their local RAAF Association branch but nothing was heard. I always thought Tom was several years older than me – both in age and wisdom – nevertheless I was very saddened when Ted Richardson found out for me that according to the records of the Royal Australian Air Force Tom died in 1976. No doubt that terrible forced march in January 1945 had a bearing on his relatively early death. So sad.

16. *Fifty Years On – Jimmy*

It was in November, 1996 that I wrote from memory what I could remember about Jimmy and it was not until the following summer that I rediscovered a collection of the wonderful letters which he had written to me at the time when we were so much in love. I referred earlier to the empty envelopes in the chapter entitled "Jimmy". I was twenty-two when they were written to me with such depth of feeling and to read them once again now that I am over eighty is an incredible experience.

I am told that such love letters are not written these days but whether this is true or not I have no way of knowing. Surely our feelings for each other still stay the same over the generations and are just as real and true; perhaps it is that the young correspond by email instead. Nevertheless, here are copies of Jimmy's letters to me and the full story of our feelings for each other. The letters I have do not begin until May after we had had an engagement party at Jimmy's home when I had been warmly welcomed into his family circle. At the end of the evening I remember as we parted to go into our separate bedrooms we thought that it was such a shame that we were still only engaged and the party had not been after our wedding reception!

We first met on Christmas Eve 1944 and became engaged in March 1945 – three months later. I even hired a wedding dress from Gainsborough Pictures in London for our wedding which we planned for September 1945 by which time we thought that Jimmy would have completed his "tour" of thirty ops with his Lancaster squadron at R.A.F. Strubby. We planned to get married at "White Lodge" my home at Saxilby, where my father still lived, and an R.A.F. Officer and his wife, from R.A.F. Scampton, lived there too and looked after him. The officer's wife, Angela, had generously offered to help with the wedding arrangements.

Shortly after being posted to his squadron to start operational flying Jimmy had to go to Louth hospital to have deadness in one of his legs investigated. This turned out to be very serious and he was transferred to R.A.F. Hospital Rauceby near Sleaford in Lincolnshire for an operation and convalescence at the Red Cross Convalescent Home at Stapleford Park near Melton Mowbray in Leicestershire and he was subsequently invalided out of the R.A.F. I believe this is now a very smart hotel or Country Club.

I wonder why I fell head over heels in love with Jimmy? I was my mother's only child although my widowed father had had four daughters by his first wife who were not much younger than my mother. At my mother's funeral, or rather after, Roo and I had gone alone together for a long walk; I told him that we must not meet again until I felt mentally stronger – as I felt very alone and in need of someone older and wiser to guide me. We had no further contact and I believed he had been killed on ops.

Ken an Australian mid upper gunner, who was with 460 RAAF Squadron at R.A.F. Binbrook, high up on the Lincolnshire Wolds was good looking, a wonderful dancer and very good natured and I was very fond of him – but not as a husband.

I met another Aussie, Tom Whiteley, and was very attracted to him as he was good company, strong in character and someone whom I could trust – but had not had time to get to know him well enough to agree to marry him before he was shot down over Germany. A couple of months or so after Tom and his crew were shot down – and with no news of him – I met Jimmy on Christmas Eve 1944.

Now, looking back more than half a century, was I feeling very vulnerable and in need of someone to love and who would love me? I really don't know.

Jimmy was determined and strong minded and our backgrounds were similar and, for a time, we were very much in love. In his letter of 1st November, 1945 Jimmy wrote a very impressive list of our differences. I like my letter to Jimmy of 10th November. I don't think I ever did find out what were "the unfortunate things he did not want to believe"!

I also think the letter to me from Uncle Ernest (Surgeon Captain E. C. Holtom, O.B.E., R.N.) is a masterly summing up of young love! I also liked the bit about Ken making tea! After having been demobbed for eight months I wrote to Jimmy – I wanted, as much as anything, to check his health was O.K. He had left Marconi and was trying to set up in business on his own. Here are the letters.

c/o Sgts Mess, R.A.F. Syerston,
Newark, Notts
Saturday 2 p.m.

My Dear Darling,

If only we knew all our nights together would be so happy as last night, before I met you I should not have thought it possible to find such happiness in one person alone but now I know at last that it is possible to build one's life around a loved one and exclude every other person in existence. Darling I know that if anything happened to you such as a disfigurement of some sort it

150

would not affect my love for you in any way. I love you my Dear one with everything that my soul, body and my mind are composed of. If only someday you will tell me seriously that you love me too I think my heart would burst through my chest, sometimes when you look at me I am sure you love me as much as I do you, your eyes Darling go so wonderfully soft and seem to be bottomless in their depth of feeling.

Did you get back safely to camp? I hope you were not too tired but it was a lovely evening after having my hopes dashed so much the previous night I only hope we will always have such wonderful reunions, don't you?

I rode back to this dump in a dream taking it easy and thinking of you, just drifting on a cloud, the boys thought I was quite mad when I arrived, it must have been the funny look in my eyes, I could not get them to focus on anything but a picture of you that was in my mind. I must close now and endeavour to work for a while.

My love to you Darling
For ever and some more
Jimmy

Sgts Mess, R.A.F. Station Strubby,
Nr Alford, Lincs
6th 3.45 11.30 p.m.

My own Dear Darling,

Fate seems to have dealt us a very cruel blow, of all places I am at least 25 miles from Lincoln. My heart almost broke this morning when I heard the news, after consulting with the rest of the crew I told the skipper we were going to see the Adj. about the posting but it was no use Darling, the Adj. told me he was very sorry but we would have to make the best of it.

The Station does not seem a bad place but however I shall exist without seeing you for may be weeks at a time I cannot imagine. My Dear Darling if only I could say this to you by the *tone of my voice you would understand how I feel about it, how much you mean to me it would be impossible to express even in spoken words but try to gather something of feeling from the poor medium of my pen. That I love you seems such a simple way to cover all the depth of emotion that the thought of you stirs in my being, my love for you fills my life to its brim, so much so I almost wonder if it is not a sin to love one person so much but nothing so beautiful could be a sin but must have come from heaven above. You said once, before you told me in words that you loved me, that if we were parted for any length of time that it would be a test for both of us to stand, but I know we have nothing to fear from such a test our love is too big a thing to fade because we are apart for a little while.*

We left Syerston at 11 a.m. this morning calling at Wadding-ton and Metheringham on the way, it was 4 p.m. when we arrived here.

God knows I cannot tell you about this place, if I was alone I am sure I could not stand it, I could not cry as once it was possible to do, but just a hard lump comes in my throat with a horrid burning sensation behind my eyes as if the tears had dried up, it would help such a lot if I could cry like a child once more, but this hurt is so much deeper it would not be cured just by tears. Being forced to go away from you seems to have taken the sun from my world, to have pulled the blind on a room, I can see no humour in anything, Darling what have we done to deserve this. Please forgive me for repeating myself but I love you so dear one, so dearly, I need you, want you with me always, so pray this war will be over as soon as possible then nothing will ever part us again.

Good night Dear heart, God keep you safe for me.

Once more be mine my love, I am yours until life's end and even death would not part us. Your scarf is going to be more to me than I thought it was possible for anything to be.

Good night, never good bye,
My love is with you always,
Vernon

> *St Mary's Vicarage,*
> *Shrubland Road, Haggerston, E.8*
> *Clissold 5484*

My Dear Bunty,

Thank you for sending me your very special news. I feel sure you will have chosen wisely, and congratulate you on your new-found happiness. I can understand a little of what you have felt during these last two years, for I know how much I miss your mother myself. She was my chief confidant, and no one can take her place; we understood one another so well.

No news of your engagement had reached me, and I was of course surprised by your letter, but not greatly so. I had an idea somehow that such an event would not be delayed much beyond the end of war in Europe,

Of course I will take the service for you if I can. I cannot <u>promise</u> because having no curate now and other matters being very uncertain. I am very much tied up. My church is not to be rebuilt, at any rate for many years, and I don't know where I shall be or what I shall be doing in the circumstances. However when the event gets nearer I shall know, and will try to arrange it.

I keep well and am very thankful bombs are a thing of the past. They were getting me down a bit. The last night we had them in London was March 27th when I was awake all night listening to a crash about once every hour. Indeed the news is most encouraging and I hope sincerely that the end will come within a month, now that the two Dictators are both dead.

The weather is horribly cold, and particularly unpleasant after the last "heat wave", but can't surely last very long at this time of the year. Every good wish to you for the future and my love.

Yrs, Ernest Wincott

The Rev. H. W. Wincott was my Mother's cousin given the courtesy title of "Uncle" as was usual in those days. As I already had a true "Uncle Ernest" I used to refer to Rev. Wincott as "Zoo Uncle" as it was he who took me on my first visit to London Zoo, introduced me to philately and the delights of fine wine and good food at Soho restaurants such as "L'Escargot Bienvenu" to which he took us on my Mother's intermittent visits to St. Thomas' hospital in London.

Sgts Mess, R.A.F. Station Strubby,
Nr Alford, Lincs.
Friday 5.30 p.m.

My dearly beloved Fiancée,

In half an hour I have to report down the flights to get my kit – just a practice stooge – now just a few lines about this place, it is a happy station, far better than most, its only snag is that it is so far away from any place, the food is good, billets not bad, huts, of course. The Gunnery Leader is a very nice type and we don't have much to do. These first dew days have been pretty hectic, getting things signed all over the place and getting new stuff, we flew yesterday afternoon, rushed a tea then flew from 6 p.m. until 1.30 a.m. Today after we got up about 11.30 a.m. Tommy and I have been changing flying kit, now after tea I am trying to tell you how much I love you in the few minutes I have left of today, I am sorry this will not get tonight's post but if I have a chance I will add some more tomorrow before I post it.

Your Uncle's letter Darling is something I had hardly dared to hope for. I am glad he approves, him more than anyone, by the way he writes to you I think he must be a very fine man.

Tommy had just told me we should get weaving so I must close but not before I tell you you are my sunshine, my world, all that I ever wish is wrapped around you, nothing could mean anything if I should lose you. I am just counting the time as it crawls by until I see you again. I only hope I shall be able to see you on Saturday. I shall certainly phone. I must go now light of my life. God bless you and keep you safe for me.

I am yours for ever then some. More than my love I send to you my very soul is in your keeping.

Vernon

P.S. I have not heard from my folks yet but then they do not yet know my address.

11.45 p.m. Saturday (?a.m.)

Sorry I can add only a few words darling, we are busy this afternoon, Tommy and I have been chasing around all morning and I am in the Post Office now. All my love again, I will try and ring you tonight.

Ward MH 2 County Infirmary,
Louth, Lincs.
Thursday 10.45 a.m. 19.4.45

Dearest One,

I was handed your letter a few moments ago and as I am soaking my foot for a while I thought it would be a good opportunity to start this as no one should interrupt me, at least for a short time. So glad you never wanted to marry any of those other guys Darling or I should have lost my chance, however, our marriage was obviously meant to be and I do agree with Mary because that is what Sue and Digger have been doing for over three years so of course now they have quite a nice little bit saved up. Darling as we are sure, what say we get married on our next leave then if I had to go abroad (God forbid) it would not be quite so hard because we could have had something of each other I hope. Darling if you agree please think up the times and places so that I can let my family know in time to get up to Lincoln for the great event, for it will naturally have to be at your home town unless you would really have it other wise because the choice of the place of marriage is always the brides. Yes dearest imagine yourself as a bride. What thrills me more is the thought of being a bridegroom, do you know the meaning of the word? The old English meaning I mean. If I should do "stinker" up so that we can be certain that she goes well, that is of course if I can get my sick leave, then scrounge all the petrol I can perhaps we would have a few days honeymoon together with some fairly good means of conveyance round the countryside, or some pretty district in the middle of which could be our hotel. Of course, funds are the main difficulty but maybe I can get over that somehow. I would like to suggest that we stayed in London for a few days and did some shows, but unfortunately that would be the most expensive way of doing things don't you agree? When perhaps with a few good films thrown in we could have just such an enjoyable time. I do hope this all meets with your approval please let me know your views on the matter. In the meantime I must get a few hints from Digger and maybe one or two from Vic. Frank's fiancée and a married friend of hers came up to see me yesterday which I thought was most kind, they were just thinking of going when Frank (that's our skipper) walked in so they stayed a little longer then all went together. Frank had been to Betty's house for her but her Mother told him she was round here so he rushed round to keep an eye on me, so he said, he knows how faithful I am really. They brought me four eggs for which I was most grateful, two oranges, some magazines, they were Everybodys, Tit Bits, The Leader and the Daily Mirror so I had something to get on with.

If you would get a copy of 'Flight' or 'Aeroplane' I shall be very grateful as I have not seen one for a long time.

So once more I must close as lunch is coming round. I will get one of the boys to post this this afternoon if they are going down the town.

With all my love once more. Saturday is only the day after tomorrow.

Yours always,

Jimmy

Ward MH 2 County Infirmary,
Louth, Lincs.
Tuesday 11.15 a.m. 24 Apl 45

Dear Darling,

I have just received your letter, another sweet letter to which I look forward so much every day.

I have thought of a lovely place to spend our honeymoon not quite so ambitious as Clovelly but just another charming place. We could also see a Shakespeare play or two, where we could take the car as it is not so far away. Darling, I am sure you can guess, Stratford on Avon. Do you like the idea my pet, it is surrounded by some beautiful country as well.

Darling I don't quite get the question about my being crewed up, I am crewed up. I have not lost my crew, I hope. If things stick to plan my leave should be sometime in August, one other thing, in a lecture from our G/C a few weeks back he said that at the end of hostilities we would get bags of leave as we should not have anything else to do so lets keep our fingers crossed. My foot should not give any trouble then, I hope it will be better in a few weeks. If you have your op, if only a month before we get married I don't think it would have any ill effect, I could look after you as well, perhaps you would ask the doc about it if you have an opp.

I think it a grand idea of yours to have your Uncle[1] and I am sure he would be very pleased. Darling you think up very charming things that's why, or one of the reasons why I love you.

Incidentally where are you thinking of having the reception as both of us have such large families – the lawn at the back of your home seems a good place with long tressel tables for the guests to sit round something like this-

---

[1] Rev. H. E. Wincott whom I had asked to conduct the marriage service

I expect Ivy would have some good ideas about it.

I love this book of H. V. Morton's so many of these places I have been to, it is most interesting, he has overlooked some things I have seen and I have missed some of his, or was too young to be interested.

My best beloved I must close now as dinner is on way.

Once more I send my love to you my dearest Darling.

So long honey child,

Yours, Jimmy

P.S. The tulips are still good but I have only 1 tart left. I love you.

40 Elmfield Terrace,
Halifax, Yorks.
3/5/45

Dearest Bunty,

When I saw your letter this morning I said "I guess this is a letter from Bunty telling me she is engaged!" We have had several of these letters just lately! So we are getting used to hearing of you young folk being engaged.

I am so very, <u>very</u> delighted about you and so glad you have written and told me. My love to you both and may you have a wonderful and happy married life together. My only sorrow is that I have never seen you although I feel I know you. Perhaps, some time we shall be able to meet – you and your husband.

Did I tell you that Rosemary, too, is engaged and they are getting married about Oct, on Frank's next leave. Frank is a Padre, and at present is in Holland. He was senior curate at our church here. He has been in the Army for 4 years now. So for the time be-

ing this will have to be their home, so we are turning things round a bit so we can give them a nice room and they can put their own things into it. What does your boy do – or want to do – in civvy life.

Kim seems to be going very well with his architecture and Michael does very well at school. He is such a worrier tho' and worries so over his homework.

When you can, please send me a photo of yourself and "Jimmy" – and let me know when the wedding is to be!

Thank you so much for writing to me and giving me the good news.

Write to me again when you can and tell me more about yourself and Jimmy.

My love to you both – bless you –
Your loving Auntie Floie[1] (Pollitt)

MH 2 County Infirmary,
Louth, Lincs.
Sunday 12.30
6 May 1945

My dearest Darling,

Did you get home safely last night without getting very wet? I do hope those lovely kisses on the stairs assured you that I love you. Strangely enough I had tears in my eyes as I went back up the stairs, silly isn't it, must have been the rain in the wind. I went into Sister's room when I came back up and talked to her for about an hour, I just had to talk to some one. I miss you so much today my Darling all I had is a memory of your eyes like two pools telling me how much you love me far more than words ever

---

[1] Auntie Floie was my Godmother. I believe she had been a student with my Mother at College. I always felt guilty because I expect my Mother had asked her to "look after me" – and I was often very neglectful in replying to her letters.

could. I also have a memory of your lips on mine and once more that shock feeling in my spine and a pulse that is racing too fast for your safety if we had been really alone. That reminds me where did you sleep last night. I wish I had broken out of here and come with you, honestly even if I don't show it you raise a very rebellious spirit in me, seems like the old green devil himself.

I do not know what time I am going tomorrow but some time and shall be going down the main road within two miles of you, if I was driving the car would turn down that road to Morton Hall as if it was automatic. As far as I can find out the place to which I am going is about four miles Newark side of Notts, but how to get there I do not know yet.

I have been up all day today although I am a little stiff. I do not seem to have suffered from our outing, I think it was a wonderful piece of luck that you came yesterday, just imagine what a bad way I would have been in without your helping hand. Where would I ever be without you? Now I have found you, existence would seem impossible without you.

I leave here tomorrow Darling your picture looks up at me with an appeal that could be 'Don't ever leave me' as if I would, as if I am ever going to give you the chance to get away from me, so your picture need not worry, but perhaps I read the picture incorrectly, perhaps you in it are just asking to be kissed or perhaps you're just asking… perhaps. Then if I look at the other photograph with its modestly down cast eyes it could be that you are looking like that because you got what you wanted. After we are married will tell you if the look was correct. I wonder.

This is possibly the last letter you will get from here depending on the time I have on Monday, I will try and get a letter off from the new dump as soon as I arrive, at least I shall be a few miles nearer you.

I am sorry my love if I am scribbling this very much but I am quite miserable today and my hand won't seem to do what I want it to, I am thinking of yesterday with you and it is very hard to spell or write. If I did not know I would see you again soon I think

160

I would sneak out when no one was looking and come over and haunt Morton Hall in company with its other ghost if it has one.

My love for always dearest please don't ever think otherwise. Thanks for a lovely day yesterday.

Yours, Jimmy

8 Brodrick Avenue.
ALVERSTOKE,
Hants.
Gosport 8398
15th May, 1945

Dearest Bunty,

So sorry not to have answered your letter sooner.

I'm very pleased to hear your news – I think Jimmie is a very nice lad – and I'm sure you will be very happy with him,

I quite agree that, as you feel sure of yourselves, there is no reason for a long engagement and I'm quite in favour of a marriage before the winter comes, so good luck to you both.

It would be nice to be married at Saxilby especially as so many of your old friends are there, and your Mummy would like it too.

Am glad to hear that Daddy had nice people living at White Lodge and that Angela is keen to help you with the wedding – of course you can have bridesmaids as well. Expect you will need the Parish hall for the reception!

Hope Uncle Ernest[1] will be able to marry you to James.

I don't know if you will be able to manage a white wedding, it is very difficult these days on account of coupons – but won't there be a scheme in the WAAFs for loaning wedding gowns? Otherwise a nice afternoon dress or smart tailor made looks well and is often useful afterwards.

---

[1] Rev. H. E. Wincott

Really Bunty, I'm very pleased to hear you've found a nice boy and are marrying soon – my love to you and a very big hug and a good long kiss.

    Your uncle,
    Ernest[1]

                    Me again,
                    Calcot,
            Reading, Berks.
            Saturday 3 p.m.
                19 May 45

My Dearest darling,

I do hope you are well I have been expecting a letter from you everyday but my luck is out, I am very worried about you Darling, I hope its just that you have been too busy to write.

I have thought about you all this week and missed you more than I can say, most evenings I have not been able to settle down to anything but have just wandered off on my own, the thing is I have nothing to play to console my lonely self.

Darling how can I tell you how much I love you, it is too wonderful for me to describe, this longing, burning inside of me that no one can stop but you, Sylvia I'm pleading now don't ever leave me my dearest.

When I think how I hurt you I just twist up inside, it seems impossible loving you as I do now I could find such a mean streak.

Mother has just been in and asked if I was writing to you and would I give you her love that goes for Dad and Isobel. Isla wants me to go up to the Green Monkey tonight but it won't be the same, you won't be with me. Perhaps you can realise how much I want to crush you close to me again and feel the glow which I always

---

[1] Uncle Ernest was Surgeon Captain E. C. Holtom, O.B.E., my mother's eldest brother.

feel passes between us like some slow burning fire that must one day consume us. Lets make it as early as possible in September my love.

My extension of leave was granted, 3 days, but I can not get back on Sunday so could I see you Tuesday night at 5.30 outside the Guard Room. I will phone you on Tuesday at 1.30 then you can tell me if it is O.K.

I am sorry I could not get through to you today my Darling, I hope you were given my message. I wish you all the luck in the world for Monday, I will keep my fingers crossed all day even if I get cramp in them.

Perhaps in a way it is a good thing I shall not see you Sunday night, as before your competition on Monday you really should have some sleep.

Good night my love.

My love is yours longer than always.

Jimmy

Ward 3 RAF Hospital Rauceby,
nr Sleaford, Lincs.
Wed. 20 June 1945

Darling,

After watching your bus go last night I walked round the corner and got a lift almost immediately.

I am very sorry something came up to spoil what had been a lovely afternoon, but after thinking it over I don't think you had any cause to get mad at me and I think that when you have thought it over what I said was quite harmless, you will agree?

After all, I don't mind if you look like an old hag because I love you very much see. I don't think you will ever be happy with me as long as I have the capacity to hurt you so easily on the other hand on your part you do get hurt very easily. It seems very ridiculous to me now that we should have had a row over such a really small matter, one day I shall have to beat your ears down hard for being so dim (because I think you're beautiful)

Its about time we both did a little getting down to suit each other don't you agree?

I hope you got home safely last night without much trouble and were not too tired. Thank you again for those lovely cuff links[1] everyone thinks they are very neat and unusual so do I.

I must stop now Darling as I have some things to do including writing to Mother, I had a letter from her yesterday, she said she had just written to you.

All my love,

Jimmy

Rauceby, Wednesday

My dearest Darling,

I am sorry but you will not get what I promised on Friday, please don't be too disappointed. I miss calculated and Saturday is my 18 day so I get up then.

I am looking forward to seeing you just the same on Friday and it will be very refreshing to see you in civvies again.

I certainly agree that a corn colour is better than ordinary blonde. I have no objections to it at all.

I miss you very much darling more so as I get bored with being in bed by myself. I do really love you very much that is another reason.

Oh boy am I cheesed. I am still progressing very well and at last am beginning to sleep better.

I must close now my Darling, sorry it is such a short note.

All my love Dearest,

Yours,

Jimmy

---

[1] I gave Jimmy a very nice pair of gold cuff links engraved with his initials.

Still Here (Rauceby)
Friday 2.15 p.m.
22 June 45

My dear Darling,

I hope you have a very good day tomorrow, go and enjoy yourself and forget me for a little while it will do you good. Give my love to Angela and her two boys.

I went to see the 'White Cliffs of Dover' yesterday I wish you had been with me, it was such a beautiful film and so very true, it had made me feel almost ashamed that I am getting my discharge, as if I was backing out of something that I was meant to do; but never mind darling I want nothing more than to live my life with you and endeavour to make you happy. Your letter was very sweet, this morning, a real love letter form your heart, I do love you so dearly. Please don't worry about your sensitivity I will try not to say things to hurt you, then I expect you will grow out of it when you get a big girl. Physically you can be as sensitive as you like, in fact the more so the better we should have more fun.

I know you love me my love I think I knew you loved me almost before you did yourself and have never doubted it once so please don't think any other way about my love for you, because it is strong as a river in flood or as an incoming tide, I only hope it is as irresistible.

I am sorry this is short darling but I have been busy this morning and the post goes at 3.15 so I must close soon not before I say again, I love my Darling, I will always love you. I hope when we are old (in years) people will say of us that we are still in love and have had happy lives. I added 'in years' because I don't think we will grow old in spirit as we both love life and things that must keep anyone young.

Good luck for tomorrow. All my love my Dearest.
Yours always
Jimmy

GAINSBOROUGH PICTURES (1928) LIMITED

STUDIOS, LIME GROVE,
SHEPHERD'S BUSH, W.12

To Mrs J S Pickering

White Lodge, Saxilby
Lincoln

11th July 1945

No. Hire 1998

The following articles have been ~~selected~~ sent to you. An ~~Official Order~~ covering the transaction will be issued in course of post.

QUANTITY	ARTICLE AND DESCRIPTION	PRICE
	White Satin Wedding Gown 64549	2 12 6
	Veil & Headdress	10 6
		£ 3 3 -
	Hire period Sept 9 - 15th 1945	

WARDROBE STORES DEPT.
CHARGE
HIRE As above
DAMAGE
TOTAL £ 3 3 -

STUDIO HIRE
SERVICE
"GAINSBOROUGH"

For use on
The hiring charges shewn above
are for run of production (but
not exceed Three Months.)

Signature

Gainsborough Pictures Invoice 11th July, 1945

BRCS Hospital,
Stapleford Park,
nr Melton Mowbray, Leicester.
(No date)

My Dearest Darling,

Since Sunday when I rung you I am once more very very much in love with you, I don't know why but last week your letter from London mentioning Ken, I was not at all sure, but I know now Darling I did love you all the time but was just a little jealous, I will always love you Dearest.

Thank you so much for the magazine, a very sweet little card and this morning two Mars bars (one of which I have already eaten) the tin of sweets and a very sweet letter.

This seems to be a very nice place with lovely grounds but it is too early yet to tell you much.

I am in a little room with W/O Sephton and Sgt Baker, remember the W/O was next to me and Sgt on the opposite side of the ward, it is very nice to be with someone one knows. I missed you so very much last week my love particularly in the dull evenings but one day rapidly draws nearer we shall be together, I only hope it comes soon.

I must close now Darling and go for a walk before lunch as exercise is essential to my getting fighting fit again.

All my love Dearest
Yours always,
Jimmy

BRCS Hospital Stapleford Park
nr Melton Mowbray, Leicester.
1st Nov 45.

My dear Sylvia,

You possibly think I am sulking or something as I have not written to you before this.

I was pleased to see you last Friday. What a pity everything went wrong so quickly, I have been thinking very hard about us here, first a few things we have <u>not</u> in common.

You are very keen on horses particularly riding. I am fond of horses but that is almost as far as it goes, anyway to go riding and come off a couple of times would be my quickest ticket to a coffin.

You do not care for car riding particularly over 40 mph. You are not the slightest bit interested in what makes a car go. I love a burst of speed now and then and as you have seen delving into the works is a very interesting ever exciting pastime of mine.

You do not get the slightest thrill listening to a symphony concert not even 'Tchaiycoski', you said so yourself. I love to listen to a large orchestra and can sit for hours with goosepimples running up and down my back completely thrilled.

You said fishing bored you and was too slow. I like fishing and find it damn good fun.

If you can add to this list as I can but have not the time please let me know, on the other hand if you think we can get over all of them when I get out of hospital eventually, and shall be longing to know that too.

I am returning to Rauceby next Monday unfortunately I shall possibly starve after the wizard food we get here.

Don't worry about coming over here next weekend as we shall only row again leave seeing me until we can go some where on our own then perhaps things will come right again.

Yours with love

Jimmy

PS Mother sends her love. My mother seems the only nice thing about me.

RAF Hospital Rauceby, Sleaford, Lincs.
Friday a.m.
9th Nov. 45

Dear Sylvia,

I think it would be a mistake for you to come over here Sunday due to the present circumstances of my being in hospital, I feel sure we should only row about the whole thing.

I heard an unfortunate thing the other day and I do not like to believe it. I hope the reason you gave in your letter for its delay was correct not that you were having a good time and possibly not time enough to write an urgent letter.

It seems a pity our engagement has gone on the rocks perhaps it can be salvaged, I will not attempt to hazard a guess until I am out of here and things are on a more substantial footing.

Yours
Jimmy

PS Please don't think I ever begrudged you a good time I have said that often enough.

426567 Cpl Pickering, J. S.
Headquarters, No. 5 Group,
R.A.F. MORTON, Lincoln
Saturday, 10th November 1945

My Dear Jimmy,

I will not come over to see you this week-end as you would rather I didn't, let me know when to arrange a meeting, and I will leave it in your hands now.

If you heard "an unfortunate thing" about me the other day which you "do not like to believe", why don't you ask me straight out instead of prevaricating? If you think it took me a long time to write to you, remember that it was no longer than the time which elapsed before you wrote after my visit to Stapleford – six days.

I most certainly have been going out a lot and enjoying my-self, but none of my actions are those of which I could feel ashamed, so should be interested to learn of this "unfortunate thing".

What would you like me to do about the ring? Shall I wear it until later on? Keep it for the time being and not wear it? Or re-turn it to you for custody? For darling, I don't want to wear it if you don't love me any more and don't trust me, so until I hear from you am wearing it on the other hand instead.

Am so sorry that this has all occurred when it is your Birthday to-morrow, for it seems so insincere to wish you a Happy Birthday under the circumstances. But I do wish you all Good Health and Happiness in the Future which is yet to come.

426567 Cpl. Pickering, J.S.,
Headquarters, No.5 Group,
R.A.F. MORTON,
Lincoln.

30th November, 1945.

Dear Sir,

I hired from you a White Satin Wedding Gown (G.4549), Veil and Headdress for the period 9th-15th September, 1945 and paid in advance the sum of £3.3/- (Draft Note 1988 of 11th July, 1945).

On the 20th August I informed you of the illness of my fiance, which necessitated the postponement of my wedding, and in your letter EB/EH/G of 24th August you kindly agreed to send me a wedding gown at some later date.

I regret to say that my fiance is still in hospital, and as I am being de-mobilised and future plans indefinite, I would be very grateful if you would kindly cancel my order and refund the charges.

I very much regret the trouble I may have caused.

Yours faithfully,

Letter cancelling wedding dress hire

Calcot,
READING.
? Dec 1945

My Dear Sylvia,

Thank you very much for Jimmy's cigarette case. I could not write sooner as I have been laid up with a very bad cold which has left me with a terrible cough, which worries me both night and day.

I was terribly grieved that you and Jimmy should part. He told me he was very hurt over your sending back his ring, he has been working on his car or he would have written to you. He gets very tired and said today that he finds he can't do as much as he used to do.

I will send your mac back in a day or two.

I hope you are well. We are all fairly well now, though I believe Jimmy is starting a cold.

Well dear, here is all the best for a Happy Christmas and though you are not to be a new daughter to me, I wish you all the luck and still pray for you to have your heart's desire.

All my love,
Yours very affectionately,
Caroline[1]

---

[1] I think this was an exceptionally kind letter to me – considering I had broken off the engagement to her son Jimmy. I note that Jimmy was "busy with his car" – so would not send a message to me via his mother!

8 Brodrick Avenue.
14 Dec. '45

My Dear Bunty,

What a surprise to fling at one without warning. Well, my dear, you should know your own affairs best, so I won't offer any comments – I expect you have discussed the matter thoroughly with Jimmy – but that just shows what a funny thing this love is.

This love is – for a period it is the only thing in the world that matters and should any one have the temerity to suggest that it might perchance be an hallucination – such a possibility would be howled out of court – Not for a moment however do I suggest that I thought it an hallucination a year ago – indeed I thought it was the real thing – as of course it was for the time.

Anyhow Bunty I am sure you have pondered the matter well and if you have come to the present decision it is much better, much better, to have done so now rather than after marriage.

By the way, does this improve Ken's chance? I suppose you still hear from him – don't forget he would get up and get your break-fast for you – that's a great point in his favour.

Well, I'm glad you are being released in January, and I see the Government are not forcing women into alternative jobs either.

I'm afraid we shall not be able to put you up for Christmas this year – we are arranging to go to St. Michaels, Shinfield, near Reading on 20 dec. till the end of the month – and that is a very small house and Elsie, Aunt Glady's sister, will be spending Christmas with us there. But I'd like to see you sometime and perhaps you could manage early in Jan – just as well to get a free travelling warrant to Portsmouth before you finally leave the service.

I don't know if we've told you anything about St. Michaels – it is Aunt Glady's little house – the tenant went out in Oct and we have moved our furniture in, and anticipate retiring there next autumn – as I have intimated I do not want to serve on after Sept. 1946.

Aunt G. has gone off to Shinfield this week end to prepare the house – I have a nasty cold, so have remained at home.

All my love and best wishes – Auntie sends her love too, and Anne is writing you on her own.

Your loving Uncle Ernest

With a kiss and hug

Sonning,

Berks.

29th January.

Dear Sylvia,

I hope your macintosh reaches you safely – Mummie has asked me to return it to you and to offer you her apologies for not having sent it back before. She has not been well for a long while – in bed on and off – for the last two months, so I hope you will accept them. Of course, my brother should have attended to it – but please excuse us all.

I hear that you are out of the R.A.F… How do you like civilian life? I expect you find it strange, but will soon become accustomed to it.

Please excuse this very short note, but I am writing it in the office, and wish to get the parcel off this afternoon so that you will be sure to receive it before Friday.

Good-bye my dear, all best wishes and luck for 1946.

Yours very sincerely,

Isla Woodley

Calcot,
Reading,
Berks.
12.8.46

Dear Sylvia,

Thank you very much for returning my brushes[1]. I had forgotten them completely,

I am pleased to hear you have realised one of your ambitions[2]. I hope things go well for you. It is very kind of you to ask me if I would like your Mother's banjo. I could not possibly accept it as a gift but perhaps I could take care of it for you until such time when you are settled in a flat or something then you may find it useful to have around for any stray musician who chanced to call.

I am sorry I have not written before this, I have been away for a few days, now I have to get down to things once more my new venture is progressing slowly.

Yours sincerely,
Jimmy

----

[1] Jimmy had left his hair brushes behind at "White Lodge"

[2] To breed a foal from my own mare Bridget

17. *The Author – Before The War*

I shall enjoy writing this section of my story for I have been rooting out long forgotten photos not seen for many a year. I want to show how the fact that I took my horse with me during my time in the WAAF was not just the sudden whim of a headstrong teenager, as horses and ponies had been an integral part of my life since babyhood.

My story begins when my mother, perhaps unwisely, went out for a drive with my father behind our keen driving pony. Taffy trotted so fast that the large yellow painted wheels of the trap spun round in a yellow blur so that the whole equipage was known locally as "The Yellow Peril". The date was Sunday, 27th August, 1922. Perhaps the drive precipitated my arrival later that day at Moorlands, Newark Road, Lincoln. In those days babies were usually born at home unless complications were anticipated.

It was not long before I declared my intention to ride. Beneath the front windows of Moorlands was a wide gravelled path between the house and the tennis court. This is where I used to be pushed out in my pram to sleep and on the following page is a photo, taken a year or two later to show the position. Here I am playing snowballs with my father. Note that despite the snow and no central heating in those days, some of the windows are open. Were people tougher in those days I wonder?

The house where I first entered the world

Snowballing on the tennis court

As mechanically propelled lawn mowers had not been invented the necessary horsepower for mowing the large areas of grass at Moorlands was provided by Taffy. Kirchen, who was a farm employee before my father retired from farming at Melton Ross in north Lincolnshire, was in charge of Taffy. As I lay in my pram I would be sure to hear the crunch of Taffy's hooves on the gravel path and the rattle of the mower behind him, followed by a short silence as Taffy would be halted in order to have his large leather over-boots fitted so that his sharp metal shoes did not damage the grass of the tennis court. Then there would be a period of noisy whirring as the grass was cut. A short silence as Taffy had his over-boots removed and then, once again the crunch of metal shoes on gravel as Taffy was led back to the stable. Usually Kirchen would stop the pony by my pram and I would be lifted out of its depths and placed on Taffy's warm back and held there safely by Kirchen until the stable was reached.

One day, for some reason, Kirchen and Taffy did not stop by my pram but completely ignored my presence. I was absolutely furious. I screamed and wept most copiously until all those within earshot came running to my pramside.

What on earth was wrong with Baby Bunting? Was she suddenly ill? Was something sticking into her? The cause could not be found. It was eventually discovered that Kirchen had not stopped that day to give me my eagerly awaited ride back to the stable on Taffy. I was absolutely furious that I had been ignored and no ride given. From then on I always tried to make it clear to adults that if any horse or pony was in range I wanted to be on it.

When my mother took me out in the pram Daisy the goat used to come along too, on a lead. However, we were banned from entry to Bracebridge Post Office after Daisy once took exception to a terrier which came in with its owner and unceremoniously tossed the dog out on to the pavement. There is no doubt that a dappled grey horse pulling a wooden cart was a favourite toy. Here I am pulling it up a steep slope from the drive to the front door of Moorlands.

On the lawn with Daisy the goat.

Bunty with her dappled horse and cart

Here I am, older, but still with the horse and cart chatting to the stone statue at the front door.

Chatting to the statue

I was three or four years old when we left Moorlands and moved to a relatively small semi-detached house in Saxilby. Presumably my four half-sisters had left home by then and Moorlands was much too large for just my parents and me. A few years ago, as I had never seen Moorlands since we left there, my husband and I went looking for it to see how the passage of time had affected it but we could not find it anywhere. Eventually we found a cul-de-sac called Chancery Close which appeared to be a relatively new development of about a dozen large neo-Georgian houses each side of a driveway entirely enclosed by some very fine trees which gave the Close complete privacy. Halfway down this road, on the western side was a huge blank brick wall of half a house. High up on a nearby wall was a plaque giving the date of 1874. This was all that remained of Moorlands. The front door and the rooms behind it had gone, as well as the stabling, greenhouses containing vines and the extensive lawns. I believe I was about fourteen years too late to see Moorlands as it used to be.

Chancery Close

Sylvia with Boolie.

The Post Mistress at Saxilby was Mrs Ford who lived in a solidly built Victorian house standing well back from the road at the lower end of the village. On the large wooden counter in the room used as a Post Office stood an old fashioned pair of scales which had a metal bowl in which to put parcels or packets to be weighed alongside which lay a row of metal weights in readiness for use. More often than not the bowl of the scales was occupied by a delightful large, long haired, grey cat who enjoyed the attentions given to her by the customers to the Post Office. She happily tolerated the rise and fall of the scales as people could not resist putting the weights on the scales to see how much the cat weighed. She was the mother of Boolie but who her father was is another question.

Our cat was always expected to stay in at night, although if it was a lovely moonlit night it was occasionally permitted to spend the night by "moonlighting" as we called it.

There was no central heating and in winter the bedroom window was often frosted over as it was so cold. Therefore, I welcomed our cat into my bedroom when I went to bed and it used to snuggle up on my bed under the eiderdown just behind the crook of my knees. Sometimes it would be permitted to come under the bedclothes and would be a nice furry hot water bottle for a time.

As I had no pony I used to dress up Boolie and harness him to a little two-wheeled cart which he used to pull on walks around the garden with me. We also used to go along the pavement outside our house for a hundred yards or so in each direction with my cat on a lead towing his little cart along, much to the surprised amusement of any passers-by. I could never understand why they looked so surprised at a cat doing such a thing. It seemed quite normal behaviour to me.

At Saxilby we had no paddock or stabling and I thought all chances of owning a pony had gone. Several times my mother found me sitting up in bed with my hands clasped around my knees, fast asleep but saying over and over again

"I shall never have a pony, I shall never have a pony, I know I shall never have a pony".

It was always with difficulty that my father could persuade me to accompany him willingly on a walk. Fortunately on this occasion I agreed to do so, for we had not long passed the vicarage when we heard the quick hoof beats of a smart pony being driven towards us. It was Mr Russon who lived a few doors away from us and used to fatten Lincolnshire Red bullocks in several of his local fields.

After pulling up his pony Mr Russon spoke to my father and told him that he had just bought a batch of ponies who were destined to go underground to work in the coal mines. One of them was too small for the task; he said I could borrow it to ride until it was sold. He would allow me to graze it in one of his fields for 5/- (25p) per week. The offer was accepted and at last, I had, temporarily at least, a pony to ride.

Naturally I was worried as to what the eventual fate of this pony might be. Happily my mother persuaded my father to buy him for me as Mr Russon had assured my father that grazing would be available. Mr Russon said the pony had cost him £10 and the share of carriage by rail was ten shillings. He wanted £1 profit. So at last I owned a pony for the princely sum of £11.10s. (£11.50).

I have often wondered why I chose the name Peterboy – Pete for short. Now I have re-discovered an old photo of a pony I rode several times whilst on holiday at Sandbanks. Across the forehead band of the bridle is a wide ribbon with the name "PETERBOY" embroidered on it. Problem solved! Now that I had a pony of my own my riding would no longer be limited to a sixpenny ride once a day whilst on holiday!

Anne and Bunty, Bournemouth. Our first visit to Sandbanks, 1928

Bunty at Sandbanks, 20th July - 3rd August, 1929

We had a long back garden at Saxilby where all our vegetables and much fruit was grown due to the efforts of my father and Kirchen who came over from Lincoln, where he did factory work, to get some peace and quiet gardening. Kirchen also attended to the acetylene machine in the brick built building designed for that purpose. This machine provided the house with lighting on the ground floor although candles were needed to light any rooms upstairs. When Kirchen was attending to its needs each week-end the smell was horrific and I found the sounds of gurgling within its interior workings quite frightening and kept well away from it.

By the time I had Bridget electricity had come to the village so acetylene lighting was no longer needed and the little brick building became my feed store and harness room.

A long narrow path went down to the hawthorn hedge at the bottom of the garden and there was a stile into the grass field beyond in which grazed Mr Spencer's dairy cows. On the far side of this was Mr Russon's field where his Lincoln Red cattle were put to fatten. Originally the area would have been two grass fields separated by a wide shallow ditch in which grew straggly old hawthorn trees. In the middle of its length was a circle of old trees which probably once surrounded a shallow pond which had long ago ceased to hold water. In both fields were numerous stumpy self sown hawthorn bushes beneath which rabbits or hares often sheltered.

I often walked over to have a chat with Pete and did not want the hassle of carrying a saddle there, so usually rode him bareback with or without a snaffle bridle. We both enjoyed jumping the stunted little hawthorn bushes but sometimes he would dodge sideways at the last moment or a rabbit would scoot out from under his feet. On these occasions Pete made a detour but I went on in a straight line. My father had warned me not to hold on to the reins when falling off as this usually resulted in a broken wrist but to let go and roll over as necessary. I had plenty of practice at this and so became proficient at relaxing when falling and not hurting myself. I am sure that this has stood me in good stead in my old age when several times I have tripped and fallen heavily on a hard surface. To the surprise of the onlookers all I have suffered is the odd bruise or two. Thanks Pete!

Surreptitiously Pete and I used to play cowboys together. We rounded up the cattle and temporarily impounded them in the clump of trees where the old pond used to be. When any of the beasts showed signs of making an escape Pete and I would canter up and turn it back to the rest of the group. Apparently Pete enjoyed this game so much that he used to play it by himself. Mr Russon complained to my father about what was happening and said that if the pony continued to prevent his cattle grazing full time another field would have to be found for him elsewhere. We both then stopped this enjoyable game.

Local children had been seen teasing Pete by throwing things at him and trying to ride him. I therefore trained the pony to rear and kick out on command if I pretended to throw things at him. This was seen by a neighbour from an upstairs window of her house. Mrs Shaw came running round to tell my mother that I was in danger of being killed by that dangerous pony! My mother thanked her and told her that on command Pete stopped his antics, gave me a kiss and had his titbits.

Sledge in Pete's snowy field

This is a photo taken on Wednesday, 28th February, 1934 of us about to have fun in Pete's snowy field. Our house can dimly be seen in the background behind me.

We had no driving harness so the clothes line provided reins and traces. A girth was used as a collar but I found it necessary to cover this with a woolly door mat taken from the foot of a bedroom door to wrap round the girth to prevent chafing. A leather girth across the back to hold up the traces completed our harness. The field was too bumpy for much fun to be had. Best of all was if there had been sufficient snow for a quiet road to be covered by an inch or two of smooth but hard packed snow where Pete's unshod feet could get a good grip. One year this was to be found past the vicarage and down the gently sloping lane towards the river Till. When turning round to come home Pete increased his speed from a steady trot into a canter. As I pulled on the reins to slow him all that happened was that I was pulled closer and closer to his flying heels – from which mini cannon balls of hard packed snow were being fired into my face. The reins had taken over the place of the traces!

I realised that we must slow down before reaching the major road by the vicarage. I saw a telegraph pole sticking up in the deep snow at the side of the road and steered Pete towards it so that the sledge runner hit the pole. That stopped us in our tracks! The clothes line traces snapped and I was dragged by the reins behind Pete for several yards face down in the snow so no harm was done. I brushed off some of the snow, knotted the clothes line traces together again and we proceeded home at a more sedate pace.

I have memories of being taken into the carthorse stable as a toddler and being lifted by the waggoner high on to the back of one of the huge cart horses whose broad back was warm for my small bare legs. As I happily sat there the stable was filled with the satisfying sounds of munching as the great animals steadily worked through their bulky feeds needed to fill those vast stomachs.

This took place on the dairy farm of Dick Stephenson who had married Joy one of my half sisters. The house is still on Riseholme Road, Lincoln which is now the busy A15. The farmland continued across to the northern edge of Sobraon Barracks on Burton Road. The farm buildings were midway between the two roads which is now covered by housing. In the photograph on the following page I am pictured, aged eight, on Daisy an ancient milk delivery pony. The farm buildings can be seen in the background on the left.

Sylvia (Bunty) on Daisy

I was permitted to be in charge of "Beaut" who was a good-natured carthorse who pulled the big metal water tank. I had to manoeuvre around several fields and place her so that I could get the tap at the back of the tank directly over the water trough at each of the large huts in which lived the big Rhode Island Red hens. They were free to roam during the day but had to be securely shut up at night to protect them from the marauding foxes who wantonly killed for pleasure and not just to get enough to eat. It was fun to collect the big brown eggs of the large hens but I was not very brave when I found a hen still sitting in her nest box. She would turn her beady eyes and look piercingly at me when I lifted up the lid. She gave me such an indignant look as I put my hand closer and closer to her. I never knew, until it was too late, whether she was bluffing or really would peck me sharply if I put my hand gently beneath her feathery body to remove her precious warm egg.

Later, when I had my own transport – Pete, I often used to ride over from Saxilby to stay. There was a fine herd of Tuberculin Tested brown and white patterned Ayrshire cows which gave lovely rich milk. The were the first T.T. tested herd in the area. As I helped drive them into the dairy from the field at milking time I gradually learned to recognise each one by name from their variously patterned coats and gracefully curving – but very sharp – horns. I enjoyed learning to milk by hand but was probably more of a hindrance than a help as I was so slow. I remember when milk bottling machinery was introduced and being fascinated by the speed with which this was done although the waxed circles sealing the top of the bottles still had to be put on by hand. I also "helped" with this task – now and again pushing the waxed discs on too hard so milk was splashed everywhere.

One thing I could do well was harnessing up and putting the milk float ponies in their carts ready for deliveries or taking them out of their carts and unharnessing them on their return. However, there was one pony, a smart hogmaned, short tailed chestnut, with a foul temper when it came to putting any harness on him. "Dandy" would either grab at you with his teeth or reach you with a hind leg. I used to bribe him with lots of tit-bits to gradually put his tack on but I rarely succeeded in getting it all on before his driver came in and completed the task. I have never met such a bad-tempered pony as "Dandy" ever since. The poor chap must have had some horribly harsh treatment at some time in his life to have made him behave in this way.

In the Spring there would be baby chicks to feed and cade lambs to bottle feed. Occasionally a flock of sheep would have to be moved. I rode Pete for this and he thoroughly enjoyed the task for if a sheep annoyed him by being laggardly he would grab hold of a mouthful of wool – and pull. The pace of the ewe would suddenly be increased and this seemed to please Pete. At certain times of the year "Rammy", the black faced Suffolk ram, would be in with his flock. If he was in with his harem you had to be wary as he was very fast, had a hard bony head and repelled all trespassers!

At harvest time I led a cart horse from stook to stook ready for the men to throw the sheaves on to the load. Remembering to call out "Hold Yer" before moving on to the next stook so the man on top of the load would not be jerked off by the sudden movement of the cart beneath his feet. I also was allowed to lead a single horse and cart with its load to the farm where the stack was being made and take back to the harvest field an empty cart in which I could ride on the return journey.

I was full of confidence with the horses and felt I understood them better than my efforts with milking and bottling. On one occasion I was in charge of two horses pulling a loaded heavy wagon and we needed to cross the Riseholme Road. It was an uphill slope to the main road and the gate posts on the opposite side of the road were not truly aligned to the first pair. My very keen lead horse, a strawberry roan named "Duke" increased speed as we approached the upward slope to the first pair of gate posts and I was very anxious not to hit the second pair as we quickly rolled down the other side of the road. I was so relieved that all had gone so smoothly. However, my relations in the house had seen it and were terrified by what they saw. I was not allowed to drive a team of horses with a loaded wagon again! I am fascinated that the five bar gate on one side of the road is there even now.

By now I had grown so tall that I looked rather large on Pete. As he had shown no objection to pulling our home made sledge we decided to turn him into a ride or drive pony. A set of harness and a tub trap or governess cart was bought for him and he was quite happy to accept his new role as a driving pony.

My mother had the bright idea that the three of us could enjoy cheap camping holidays together. However, his behaviour was unpredictable when faced by lorries, vehicles with flapping loads or tractors and I usually had to jump out and hold him until the terror had passed. We went to Derbyshire for a week and here we are all ready to set off. Note the tent and kettle slung beneath the trap.

Pete ready for camping

We cooked our meals on an open fire or a Primus stove if it was wet and it all tasted wonderful – particularly pancakes.

When we arrived at the Bridge Inn, Calver and asked if we could camp in his paddock alongside the River Derwent the proprietor, an ex-policeman, Mr R. Heathcote, quizzed my mother as to whether we were selling anything – which was hardly surprising! We camped there from 1st-5th June, 1934 and once it was known we were not gypsies were made most welcome. Here I am showing Peter he can paddle in the Derwent and have a good drink or cool his feet at any time.

Pete cooling his feet

Pete came over to the tent to give me a good morning kiss

We wanted to visit Matlock and with some difficulty found a field at Ambergate where we could camp and Pete graze whilst we went into the town for the day by bus. My father regularly used to visit that Spa town in order to "take the waters" and told us of beautiful gardens there. When we returned in the evening the air felt very thundery and we were both weary as we made out way up the hill to the field. I got there first but to my horror could see no signs of a tent. I alarmed my mother by calling out excitedly "It's gone, everything has gone!" Due to the slope of the ground and the fact that Pete had felt lonely and in need of some titbits he had completely flattened the tent in search of them for himself. He had opened and sampled any containers which interested him – cornflakes, butter, flour, eggs were spread everywhere. The precious half pound block of Cadbury's Dairy Milk had probably been his most enjoyable find. So many of the tent tapes had been ripped off the tent pegs could not be put into place again until my mother had done a lot of sewing that night. Whilst the thunder and lightning rumbled in the distance, Pete stood at the far side of the field watching, knowing that he was in disgrace. The tent was just re-erected before the rain came down. Thankfully there was just one tin that Pete was unable to open as it had a very tight fitting lid. That contained my favourite chocolate wholemeal biscuits...

We had planned to spend another night camping on our way home but aided by all the goodies he had stolen the previous day and the gradual slope of the ground towards Lincolnshire we made such good time that there seemed no point in stopping. We were back home by tea time and when Pete had been unharnessed he enjoyed a lovely roll on the lawn in the back garden. If we ever left a camp site again we were determined never to leave Pete and the tent alone together.

The following year we planned to go camping in Yorkshire for a fortnight. As the Humber Bridge had not been built we had to cross the river at Goole. On the way there we stayed on land at Lawn's Farm, Epworth on the Isle of Axholme for the night of Wednesday, 12th June, 1935.

Mr and Mrs Lee with Winnie, George and Ralph at Lawn's Farm.

We went through Beverley calling in to go round the lovely Minster and then on to the coast at Barmston. We wanted to stay the night near Pocklington. Incredibly I can still remember my mother asking a woman if she would let us stay on her land. This woman, wearing an apron and rubbing her hands together in a miserly fashion, said in a croaking voice "How much can you afford to pay? How much will you pay?" We neither paid or stayed but the memory still lingers on.

On the back of the above photo my mother wrote: What are the wild waves saying? Bunty and Pete at Barmston, Yorkshire-Saturday, June 15th 1935 camping. A mid-day rest with lunch, leaving trap on cliff.

At lunch time we always took off all Peter's harness and put a head collar on him instead so that he could enjoy grazing at the roadside whilst we too had something to eat. Pete also had a drink of water and was brushed down. He usually decided to have a vigorous roll on the side of the road, his hind quarters often getting covered with dust from the edge of the road. The occasional passing motorist looked askance at his antics, probably not knowing whether he was in extreme pain or merely enjoying himself.

Barmston, Yorkshire 15th June, 1935

We went up along the coast as far as Sandsend just north of Whitby and were greatly looking forward to driving across the North Yorkshire Moors to Pickering from whence my ancestors probably originated. The road from Sandsend to Pickering was very hilly and so we had to spend most of the day walking beside Pete in order to lighten his load uphill and make the descent easier for him in order that he did not slip. It rained all day long and it was so misty we could not admire the views. By the time we reached our destination we were soaked through and that was the only occasion when we had to seek bed and breakfast accommodation for the night in order to dry out.

We wanted to visit York and had a delightful campsite and welcome at Heslington by Mr Connel, Barbara and Jack from Friday, June 21st to Tuesday, June 25th 1936

In 1936 we spent three weeks camping in Norfolk but had difficulty in finding anywhere to stay as the Lincolnshire Fens were so highly cultivated that little grazing was available. From Kings Lynn we followed the coastline and had a particularly enjoyable stay at a field from which we could see Castle Rising. Another memorable time was at West Runton near Cromer. We visited Castle Acre and the Broads taking a cruise from Potter Heigham.

Those were memorable holidays which could not be repeated these days. Never once was Pete unwell or lame in all the time I owned him.

The year 1936/37 was spent at Boarding School in Ambleside.

Camping on Cat Bells near Derwentwater with Miss Doreen Hickling, our Guide Leader, in the centre (Sylvia on the right)

When I returned home after a year at Boarding School it was obvious that I had outgrown my beloved pony Pete whom I had had since he was a five year old.

Presumably my mother was taken into my father's confidence when he decided he would find a horse for me to ride. I knew nothing of this. One day he announced he had bought a 15.1 h.h. bay mare for me from a smallholder at North Scarle. My mother was worried. "Surely not that hot-headed little mare?" she said. The deed was done. I had never even set eyes on the mare before she was delivered to White Lodge – let alone sat on her!

I lost my little garden as a stable for Bridget was built over it. Now that electricity had come to Saxilby the brick building which had housed the acetylene lighting apparatus became my storage space for hay/straw. The smaller part was used for my tack and short feed.

In the winter it was lovely to be able to look out of my bedroom window and see Bridget looking out over the stable door. She particularly enjoyed a pie dish of sweetened tea when we had our elevenses but spilt a lot as her tongue was smooth and lacked the bristly roughness which enables cats to drink so neatly.

We had a lot of fun at local shows and gymkhanas put on in aid of the Red Cross. Bridget was too big to be any good at Bending Races. She was fast at Potato Races – but I usually missed the bucket in which I had tried to throw the potato. Musical Chairs was often a winner unless we had to dismount and run in each time to stand on our sack marker. Bridget became so excited the longer we were still "in" that she became very difficult to mount. Local show jumping was fine unless the "professionals" turned up with a lorry load of proper show jumpers. Section Jumping, in which teams of four raced round the ring as fast as possible, and in line, was our forte. Bridget could trot at about 20 m.p.h. and was nearly unbeatable. I still have a silver table napkin ring won at Scothern Gymkhana in memory of her success there.

When riding as a group with friends they usually asked to have a ride on her but, if let out of a trot, Bridget bolted with us all in turn – as she was determined to impress all and sundry she "was the leader of the pack!"

At Saxilby Show proudly displaying four rosettes won that afternoon.

Outside Stow Church

The above photograph taken outside Stow Church shows me vainly trying to get Punch to turn round and face the camera. My mother has written on the back of it "Jan. 1939" Note my old Whippy saddle had a linen lining so lots of tack cleaning needed. No easy way out by using a numnah in those days! If Punch became tired on our outings together and began to lag behind I stopped Bridget. If he wanted a ride Punch would come up to Bridget, stand up on his back legs against her foreleg and I would reach down to pull him up to ride in front of me on the saddle.

It was my cousin Denis who traced Bridget's army origins for me when he was at Sandhurst. In January, 1939 he came to stay with us and we rode out together. He also took me to my first formal dance at the Assembly Rooms in Lincoln which was a truly memorable occasion for me. Denis was killed on the beach at Dunkirk. I believe he had been an M.T. Officer with the East Yorkshire Regiment but I am not sure.

My cousin Anne's parents were in Malta as her father was in the Royal Navy there. It was arranged that during Anne's holidays from Boarding School at Easter 1939 my mother would take us both out to visit them. Time was limited so we went overland by rail, taking three days and two nights for the journey, sleeping on the train en route. I doubt if Malta possessed an airport for civilians in those days – anyway it would have been far too expensive. By sea the journey would have taken far too long. I remember we stopped in Paris only long enough to change stations. In Turin we had time to have a meal of goat stew in the town. Waking up at dawn we crossed the Alps with the sun rising and casting a pink glow on the snowy slopes. For much of the route from Rome southwards the rail track ran close to the sea with gorgeous views. Mussolini had recently travelled the same way so masses of flags and banners everywhere proclaimed his popularity. Bedspreads and brightly coloured towels were draped from every possible open window. The atmosphere was tense.

In order to cross the Straits of Messina to Sicily our train was put on a boat for the crossing and passengers could alight and wander about the deck. There were numerous troops on board and the carabiniere were proudly lounging around displaying their patent leather tricorne hats adorned with a plume of feathers. My mother warned us both to keep a straight face as we were still of an age when a fit of the giggles could easily consume us and my mother was worried lest we upset anyone by our hilarity.

On reaching Sicily we boarded the train again and went down to Syracuse and from there on to Malta by steamer. The return journey was done in the same manner.

It was not long after this that I remember squatting to reach into every corner in our two attics busy with lime-wash to paint all the woodwork to lessen the fire risk in case of incendiary bombs falling on the house. I had by now completed my secretarial training at Lincoln Technical College and had also reluctantly attended evening classes in French and German.

I enjoyed a temporary Civil Service post at the R.A.F. Recruiting Centre at Newport Barracks in Lincoln. This was soon followed by another job at the Employment Exchange in Lucy Tower Street, Lincoln trying to decipher hand-written reports of tribunals for those who did not wish to be called up to serve. The handwriting of the tribunal report was extremely difficult to decipher and I was supposed to answer the switchboard too. I remember it as a depressing, smelly building whose windows were criss-crossed by brown paper strips to minimise damage if shattered. A brick wall had been built outside the window which obscured most of the light. I was thankful when I was no longer needed and so volunteered for service in the WAAF. At that time one could not enlist until the age of eighteen although by June, 1941 this had been lowered to seventeen-and-a-half. I volunteered to join the WAAF on the 27th August, 1940 – my eighteenth birthday but was not called up until the first of January, 1941.

If you have read thus far, you will realise that it was not the whim of a teenager to take her horse with her when she joined the WAAF. I could not leave Bridget behind and there was a very good chance that my postings would be within the county as there were so many airfields in it – we were not called "Bomber County" for nothing.

18. *The Author – After The War*

I was demobbed on 8th January, 1946 and returned home to look after my father. Although I had got Gay Boy to ride I realised that he would not be suitable for me to take down to Porlock to Tony Colling's posh Riding School for my unexpected place on Major Jed O'Dwyer's top show jumping course. Therefore, I looked in 'Horse and Hound' and found what sounded to be a most suitable horse for sale at Quedgeley in Gloucestershire. The dealer often advertised horses called "Aaron's something or other". This ensured a billing at the top of the alphabetical list of horses for sale! This one was called "The Lad" a big liver chestnut gelding with a Roman nose – often the sign of a puller. I went to see him and bought the horse for a hundred guineas and renamed him "Final Folly" for if I had made a mistake I should never be able to afford another horse. Folly came up to Saxilby by rail. Not long afterwards when Leslie was staying with us I remember him helping to load us both on the train to travel down to Porlock for the course.

The railway line only went as far as Minehead and Folly and I disembarked from the train onto the platform amongst all the passengers and their luggage. I then had to saddle up and ride the next seven or eight miles to Porlock on the road but traffic was still minimal as petrol rationing remained in force.

Show Jumping Course, Porlock. I am pictured on Folly second from the left next to Col Harry Llewellyn who formed the famous show jumping partnership with Foxhunter. Major O'Dwyer is standing in front of us.

We all had to use snaffle bridles so I was lent one for Folly instead of the double bridle which he normally wore. I was constantly being told to sit up straight and keep my shoulders back which was virtually impossible for me to do as Folly pulled so hard.

Major O'Dwyer thought I could do well with a more suitable horse and said he would see what he could find for me on his return to Ireland but that Folly was quite unsuitable for me to make into a show jumper.

I knew of a very pretty lightweight grey gelding "Mickey Mouse" who was ridden poorly in local show jumping classes by a youth, therefore, I rode several miles away to visit his owner Mr W. who farmed near the river Trent as I wanted to see if I could buy the horse. Mr W. would not sell Mickey but liked Folly so much that he bought him for ten pounds less than I had paid for him. I was thankful that I had lost so little on the deal.

A few weeks before Folly was sold I took both him and Gay Boy to a little show at Saxilby. By now both horses were besotted with each other and hated to be parted. I was in the ring jumping Folly and across the arena Gay Boy was being held and he whinnied to Folly. Folly replied by bolting with me towards his friend and cleared the arena rope, luckily without damaging himself or spectators. He was really a man's horse!

By now Gay Boy had been so well trimmed and groomed that I sold him that day at the show for fifty pounds to a young fellow who admired him and wished to buy the horse. As the horse had cost thirty-five pounds a few months previously I was pleased to make a profit this time. However, I did hear that the purchaser was disappointed later on when he had had time to discover how hairy Gay Boy would become if not expertly trimmed. Rather in the same way that a smartly trimmed poodle would look when trimmed by a professional and then left untrimmed for a few months.

Whilst Leslie was staying with my father and me at Saxilby in June Leslie and I decided to go into Lincoln by Hutson's bus (6d. single, 10d. return) to buy some Walpamur paint to decorate the very shabby bathroom. On our return we were shocked to discover that my father had unexpectedly died and so my half-sister Ivy generously welcomed me to her home at Leadenham to live or I could stay with Elsie, another half sister, on her little farm. White Lodge was let furnished.

True to his promise Major O'Dwyer wrote to say he had found me a very promising chestnut mare he considered suitable for me in Ireland. I had to write back and explain that my circumstances had now changed due to the death of my father and I would have to find a job.

Leslie and Sylvia on Waterloo Station, July, 1946.

I heard that a Mrs C. was wishing to start a riding school at Weelsby Park in Grimsby where the Old Hall had burnt down but the fine stables remained. Mrs C. had little experience in that direction and I now urgently needed a full time interesting challenge to keep me fully occupied after the shock of my father's sudden death. So I took on the task of creating a successful riding school and livery business and also doing the teaching. We charged five shillings for an hourly lesson or on a two hour ride for ten shillings we could get as far as the beach at Cleethorpes where we usually enjoyed jumping the breakwaters if the tide was right.

I began teaching at 9 a.m. and finished at 9 p.m. after giving Mrs C. private tuition for an hour.

I wanted to go to the local Hunt Ball and invited Leslie to come up to escort me. When he came he was shocked to find me looking so tired and he stayed on to help. By this time we had also become, at the request of those dog owners who rode with us, somewhere that they could leave their dog in safe hands whilst on holiday. Mr Slinger, our helpful local vet, wanted us to become quite big with kennels and runs being built in addition to holiday accommodation as it was envisaged that we should also provide the kennels for dogs impounded by the police.

I must also tell you about one amusing incident. On the far side of the little stable yard, in the centre of the wall beneath the Clock Tower, was a narrow stone staircase which led up to two large rooms over the stables in which our hay was stored. One busy Sunday, we came back from lunch ready to saddle up for the 2 p.m. ride. "Flicka" the old chestnut ride/drive horse had got loose, gone up the narrow stairs and was looking out of an upstairs window! We rugged him up, bandaged his legs, put on knee pads, covered the staircase deeply with straw and put a rope around the horse's chest to hold him back in case he slipped and fell down the stairs. It took us ages to do all this. Happily it was all unnecessary as the old horse walked down the staircase as if he were used to doing it every day of his life without so much as a faltering step.

The winter of 1946/47 will long be remembered for the intensity of the cold and the depth of the snowdrifts. It was no longer a pleasure to hack along the beach at Cleethorpes as the wind was bitter and the sea water froze in the shallows. However, some exercising still had to be done as we now had ten or twelve horses and ponies stabled.

Due to the terrible weather no horses or ponies could be let out for hire and we had no such luxury as an indoor school. Our business was no longer viable and our partnership ended. I sent my ex-police horse, Bala, and Kerry Piper, a horse which my friend June had lent me, to Louis Furman's racing stables nearby as boarders. Leslie and I went out there to exercise them in the snowy fields until the railway line to York was cleared and both horses were able to be sent to York Horse Sales to be sold. Louis told me that Mr W. S. Lockwood, MFH was looking for a rider for his son's horse, H.M.S. Sturgeon, in a Ladies' Point-to-Point Race once the thaw came. This was a good horse who had once beaten the famous steeplechaser Prince Regent but had become soured by hard steeplechase races, so the owner wanted to try the horse in a more lightly weighted Ladies' Race at a Point-to-Point. What a wonderful chance this would make for me.

I am not sure why I longed for the chance to ride in a point-to-point race. Perhaps it was because, as a child, I had watched my half sister Elsie Pickering ride in Ladies' Races on her old steeplechaser Irish Flyer. I imagined it would be a wonderful feeling to gallop over safe, purpose built, big black fences for three miles.

However, when hunting Bridget I always had to ride her steadily at a fence. It was impossible to know until the last moment whether I might have to stop suddenly because I had just seen nearly invisible barbed wire on posts away from the hedge to stop cattle pushing their way through it. Or there might be a set of harrows or other piece of farm machinery on the landing side which I would need to avoid. My father used to follow the hunt in his car. In the evening he would go over the events of the day and often say "I saw you crossing the field at so-and-so; why didn't you let Bridget gallop on?" My reply was always the same "Daddy, if I had let her go at full speed, I couldn't stop her". Therefore the idea of really galloping over safe ground for three miles where there was no barbed wire or other hidden dangers sounded wonderful to me!

I treasure a race card of the Burton Steeplechases at Walesby held on Monday, February 10th, 1902 price sixpence.[1] There were only two races and my father had an entry in each of them. The first race was at 2.30 over three miles. A silver cup was presented by Mrs Wilson, added to a Sweepstake of £1 each. Beside the entry "Mr T. Pickering's b. g. LADDIE". My father had pencilled in "second". (eleven entries).

The 3.15 was a FARMERS' RACE of three miles. The winner £8, second £2 added to a sweep stake of ten shillings each.[2] There were seven entries. My father entered a roan gelding PEAT. I know he rode over some huge fences on his own farm but he never mentioned that he rode in races himself so his horses were probably ridden by someone else.

----

[1] 2½p

[2] 50p

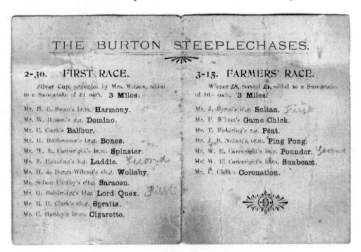

Burton Steeplechases Race Card

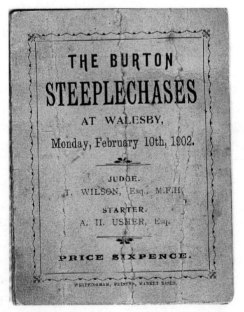

Burton Steeplechases Race Card Cover

Fortunately the snow cleared in time for the South Wold Point-to-Point races to be held on 17th April, 1947 when I had my first ride in the Ladies' Race at the Spilsby course. I was very apprehensive as never in my life had I ridden at racing pace, approximately thirty miles an hour, over a fence of any size. How ashamed I should be if I fell off at the very first obstacle for I should never be given the chance of race riding again as no one would ask me to ride their horse in case I fell off it.

Ladies' Races are usually run faster than those for men. It is not always realised that this is because it is the horses, not the riders, who decide to start the race at a tearaway pace and it is very difficult for one of our sex to steady their mount when the flag is dropped. If one or two horses take command of their riders and set off in the lead the race will be lost if they are given too much start. Nevertheless, Sturgeon had had a lot of hard races with men riding him and as a result was soured by steeplechasing. It was hoped that by having a stone less to carry in a Ladies' Race at a Point-to-Point and the fact that I would not use my whip on him might just persuade him to run well.

Nevertheless I thought that I was wonderfully fortunate in having the chance of riding an experienced horse, who was a safe jumper, for my first race ride on that cold and blustery day.

In case I fell off I did not fancy other horses trampling on me so was about last over the first fence and was delighted to find that the partnership was still intact when we landed. After a few more fences I began to enjoy the exhilaration of it all and chatted confidingly to Sturgeon as we raced on together. Sensibly I did not try to dictate to him how he jumped but left him to make his own decisions in his own time. Having done quite a lot of show jumping I found that this was helpful as I could see whether or not we were meeting a fence on a good stride from several lengths away and whether he would be easy to sit on or not when he jumped it.

I was surprised to find that I was in front approaching the last fence and suddenly realised that I had not bothered to check exactly where the winning post was as I had not anticipated that its position would greatly concern me.

All of a sudden there was the sound of a horse brushing through the top of a fence close behind me and a chestnut nose appeared at my girth. It was that of Jan King who was giving Lady Wendy Pelham her first race ride. I am happy to say that Sturgeon and I won by a length. In the local Press it was reported that "honours of the day went to the ladies in the town open nomination when Miss Pickering won for the first time, being only a length ahead of Lady W. Pelham on Jan King."

	Owner	Horse	Rider
1st	Mr W. A. Lockwood	H.M.S. Sturgeon (Burton)	Miss S. Pickering
	Distance: 1 length	Price: 5/1	
2nd	Mr D. Burt	Jan King (Brocklesby)	Lady W. Pelham
	Distance: 8 lengths	Price: 3/1	
3rd	Mr W. Ransom	Tartan's Gift (Blankney) Price: 6/1	Miss J. Nelstrop

In third place was Joy, the daughter of my half-sister Ivy.

The following year I rode Sturgeon again but disgraced myself by falling off him when he pecked (stumbled) a couple of strides after landing over a fence when he trod on a stone. I won't go into my feelings – nor that of his owner. It is not surprising that I was not invited to ride the horse again.

I am being led out on H.M.S. Sturgeon. The owner, Mr. Arthur Lockwood, is on the left.

The same season I rode Mr Donald Burt's, M.F.H., horse "Jan King". Prior to that race Mr Burt arranged for me to jump a circuit of Market Rasen Steeplechase Course one day after racing had taken place to see how Jan King and I got on together. Jan King was a very broadly built horse and I never felt I could get a really good grip on him if things went wrong. Luckily all went well and I was pleased to be second to the more experienced pair of Ann Haxby and her horse "Out of Favour".

Richpool was the third of the trio of horses I rode in races. He was owned by Mr J. Baker who had sold Bridget to my father several years previously.

Ladies' Point-to-Point - Sylvia on Richpool.

A week or two before I was given the ride another girl had been riding Richpool in the Blankney Hunt Ladies' race when he was the hot favourite. I am told that Richpool was in the lead as he approached the last fence but suddenly slammed on his brakes and refused to jump it. Thank heavens I was not riding him that day for that would have definitely been the end of my race riding career! I rode Richpool in three races. On one occasion another rider, who was reputed to need strong liquid refreshment before she rode in a race, crossed in front of me as we approached a fence and so we were unable to jump it. However, I did have a win on him when I beat my half sister Elsie Pickering into second place when she was riding her own horse "Orton Scar" which she had trained herself.

I also had a second place on Richpool but I don't remember the details. Our final race took place on Easter Saturday in 1949 at the Grove Point-to-Point when we did not complete the course as he suddenly decided he had had enough of racing and refused to jump another fence with me.

My total of race rides was seven in three seasons, gaining a total of two firsts, two seconds, an "unseated rider", a "run out" and "a refusal".

Leslie was very pleased when I moved out of the county for my next job as he did not enjoy watching his fiancée race ride because of the risks involved.

For a short time I took a job at the Filey Butlin's Camp where I issued tickets to holiday makers who wished to ride and hired out jodhpurs as needed.

I then went to work for Mr W. E. Livings at Munden Stud Farm in Hertfordshire taking young Red Wine with me by train. I travelled with Red in the Groom's Department adjoining his stall and could see and chat to him through a small connecting window. I was surprised how quickly Red judged from the noises around him that the train was about to pull up. On hearing the sounds of the brakes being applied he would take a couple of steps backwards and press his hindquarters against the end wall so that the change of speed did not put him off balance when the train stopped.

Mr Livings had a piebald pony at the farm which I started on his jumping career and I am told that he subsequently became a well known show jumping pony called Munden Magpie.

That autumn I went to live-in and work as a groom for Mr Keith Wright at The Rookery, Fenstanton in Cambridgeshire. It was a very comfortable home where I lived with the family. They had an excellent cook who showed me how to make choux pastry as éclairs were a particular favourite of mine! I was expected to have completed my work and be changed out of riding clothes and be clean and tidy by the time we had a very nice tea together. Mr Wright rode a big bay gelding "Huntsman" and his son Ian a chestnut show hunter named "Page Boy". I introduced their ex-hurdler "Easy Row" to hunting and jumping strange obstacles at various speeds instead of only jumping hurdles at racing pace. I was also in charge of a well-bred brood mare named "Applause". She was a boarder who was in foal, stabled at night but grazing in the field during the day. She had a lovely foal whilst I was there. Shortly afterwards "Applause" and her foal went to H. M. the Queen's Wolferton Stud at Sandringham in Norfolk.

Easy Row, Red Wine and Huntsman grazing in the Spring

Red Wine came with me and I can remember backing him, or getting on his back for the first time. I was by myself and decided that it might be safer to do this outside rather than in the stable so took him into the stackyard for the experiment. I thought there would be more space there in which to fall safely if he played up. All went well. He stood as good as gold. By now Leslie was studying at the London Foot

Hospital to become a State Registered Chiropodist and we often spent time together in Cambridge on my day off.

In the Christmas holidays when the children were back from boarding school Mrs Wright went up to London to do some shopping. It was a wet day and in the evening streets glistened in the rain and headlights were dazzling. Mrs Wright was tragically killed when she looked the wrong way when crossing a one-way street. It was not long after this that I left.

Sylvia on Dr. C.A.N. Hick's "Sporting Chance" takes a water jump at Huntingdon County Show

Dr and Mrs C. A. N. Hicks had been out hunting and Mrs Hicks had seen me there, liked my style and the way I handled Easy Row. They invited me to go to live-in and work for them at Huntingdon. The doctor had his practice there and they kept several horses and ponies on the grazing land by the river Ouse. There was stabling for four horses at their home. They had a most helpful Polish couple who lived in. Alfred did all the grooming, mucking out and tack cleaning whilst his wife, Vera, attended to the chores indoors. Lavender always fed the horses herself. I did all the exercising, schooling and competing.

Mrs Hicks, or Lavender as we always called her, used to cook the main course for our mid-day meal and I experimented and became proficient in preparing the sweet course. I also taught myself how to bake nice things for tea, especially for tea parties when people came to play tennis and if they had a dinner party I was responsible for the sweet course. I even went to dress making classes for a short time.

Sylvia and Nimrod at Hunter Trials

Many weekends Leslie would take a train to Huntingdon and stay in a B. and B. close by for Friday and Saturday night. We would then have the whole of Saturday and Sunday together until the evening when Leslie returned to Town to continue his studies. In winter two of the four internal loose boxes were occupied by Dr Hick's "Sporting Chance" a big hunter and his old ex-Army horse "Nimrod". The other two were taken up by "Danny" who was supposedly bought for Lavender to ride and my young "Red".

Late on cold wintry nights Leslie and I used to enjoy going down to the stables close by to say good-night to them. They were warmly rugged up and contentedly dozing or picking at their hay nets. Red was often lying down in his deep straw bed but when we switched on the electric light he did not bother to stand up. We used to creep quietly into his loose box and squat beside him so that we could stroke him gently and chat to him. Red would give soft little grunts to us as his reply. We would then creep out of the box again, close the door quietly, switch off the lights and retire to our own beds.

We were treated as members of their family and we all ate together and could ride any of their horses or take their boat out on the river Ouse which flowed at the bottom of their garden.

Sylvia with Saffron and Beauty Queen. River Ouse, Summer 1949

Dr Jim would always offer us a drink when we came in from riding and we were often their guests for dinner at the Bridge Hotel which was nearly opposite.

I found Lavender had an old side saddle so I taught her horse, Danny, to carry it and myself to ride on one. Danny used to spook a lot when we rode near the river Ouse on the wide grassy Common of Portholme. He would often half rear and try to spin round and was very quick on his feet.

Sylvia and Danny on Castle Hill.

Sylvia on Red Wine (rising 5 years), Portholme Common, March 1949.

Sylvia with Red Wine in a water carrying race at a Gymkhana

Now that Leslie had become a fully qualified State Registered Chiropodist it was time for us to get married and find somewhere to live.

Leslie's favourite photo of Sylvia, which he took abroad with him.

Leslie, Sylvia and Saffron outside the Church at Huntingdon.

Dr Jim and Lavender generously offered to let us be married from their home and our wedding took place just before Christmas, 1950. It was almost exactly ten years since Leslie and I had first met on a snowy, bitterly cold night at that village dance hall in Market Overton when we were both reluctantly persuaded to venture out that night.[1]

The intervening years had been kind to me but Leslie had endured much during his time in North Africa, Italy and Yugoslavia but he will not let me tell his fascinating story.

Dr. Jim was Leslie's Best Man and I was given away by my Uncle, Surgeon Captain E.C. Holtom, RN. In the photograph outside the Church we are being greeted by Saffron, a yellow Labrador bitch they gave us as a wedding present.

----

[1] The story of this meeting was told in my previous book

Red, Sylvia and Saffron.

I am told that Bosworth House, stables and gardens have now been swept away due to the construction of a big new bridge over the River Ouse.

After we married we lived near Sittingbourne in Kent for four years. We then moved to Berkhamsted in Hertfordshire which was just under thirty miles from London between Watford and Aylesbury where the Chiltern Hills offered lovely country for walking or riding.

I applied for a full time job as secretary at Ashlyns School on the hilltop above the town and was pleasantly surprised when I got it. I think my application was helped by my R.A.F. form 1250 Service and Release Book for it stated "This airwoman has been employed in the Defence Section for the last one-and-three-quarter years. She is a very reliable shorthand-typist and a correspondence clerk above average standards, quick, able and trustworthy." I remained in the post for over twenty years until I was able to take slightly early retirement.

Ashlyns School, Berkhamsted.

The vast impressive buildings were originally built by the Thomas Coram Foundation for Children as a boarding school. Not long after I started work there it was bought by the Hertfordshire County Council and became Ashlyns School. The architect of the school had also designed the R.A.F. Staff College, Cranwell. If you are familiar with the latter you will note how similar they are in the appearance of their frontages.

226

Sylvia and Leslie enjoying a well earned holiday abroad in 1960.

The longer I sit looking at these old photographs of horses and ponies the more memories of each of them come flooding back to me. There is now a whole group of them in my mind's eye, all asking to be mentioned. I have already given my memory a free rein for far too many pages. I must now be ruthless and let very few push open the gate from memory to print. All the rest must go back to graze again in the fresh green pastures of my memory.

Whilst living at Berkamsted I had great pleasure in riding Welsh Cobs and Anglo-Arabs for a friend at numerous shows. I think the greatest enjoyment was obtained as a result of buying Tracy, a part-bred Arab mare and Sundown her foal at Newbury Arab Sales. They had been placed third and first in their respective classes at Watford Horse Show that year. They both went up to my half-sister, Elsie Pickering, to grow-up on her farm and I would go up and visit them during school holidays. Elsie said foals did better if they had a companion of their own age so I bought a Fell/Thoroughbred colt foal, John Courage, from Mrs E. Polling at Bovingdon to keep Sundown company. I continued with their education when they came down to Berkhamsted as three year olds.

Sarah Halling with John Courage

John Courage was purchased by Sarah Halling. In due course he changed hands and had a very successful career in Working Hunter Show Pony classes all over the country, as well as winning Side Saddle classes. I believe his name was changed to "Just J".

Elizabeth Cliff on Sundown, September 1978

Sundown was sold on as a three year old, was much loved and lived out his life in luxury at his home in Richmond Park until he developed Cushing's Disease at the age of about twenty.

From Tracy we bred two further foals – Ashlyns Sunrise and Ashlyns Sunbird. The sire of the two foals was the Arab Stallion Cochise (Starguard/Magic Dream) as by then I had known and ridden both Arabs and Anglo-Arabs sufficiently to enjoy greatly their sometimes quirky characteristics. They are much like thoroughbreds who like you to ask them to do something for you. They resent attempts to dominate them but will usually co-operate willingly if asked – rather than ordered to do your will. Cochise was well bred, good looking and was available locally.

Bridget Clark with Tracy.

Cochise, 1974

Sunrise was the first foal we bred from Tracy by Cochise. From a young age he looked like his father in appearance and already had his strong likes and dislikes. It was planned to take mare and foal to the Lincolnshire County Show. In order that they could have some practice in being led, Tracy and Sunrise were moved out of the field which contained other mares and foals. Sunrise took exception to this. He left his mother and jumped a post and rail fence to re-join his foal companions.

Ashlyns Sunrise at ten weeks old, Whitsun 1975

When it came to the day of the show we were trying to put whitening on his white socks. He objected to this so strongly that he quickly stamped up and down with the whitening ending up on his hoof rather than his sock.

Dr Anthony Thompson let us keep Sunrise in his paddock and stable at Little Gaddesden. In the photograph Leslie and Sunrise are enjoying a quiet walk together down Princes Riding towards the Monument. Leslie is wearing a tabard stating 'CAUTION – YOUNG HORSE'.

Leslie on Sunrise as a three year old

Leslie and I enjoyed hacking Sunrise in the lovely wooded bridleways where, much to Sunrise's delight, deer or squirrels might pop out at any moment giving him an excuse to spook. Sometimes Leslie would become confused by all the different pathways and would not be sure which was the one to take to get back to his starting point. If this happened all he had to do was drop his reins and leave the navigation problem to Sunrise. It never failed.

Carren Smith-Hughes rode Sunrise at Northfield Grange Hunter Trials in 1981 when he was a six year old. This was the first time he had ever been asked to jump a fixed telegraph pole.

Carren Smith-Hughes competing on Sunrise

Tamara on Sunrise 16th April 1984.

In the photograph above, Tamara, Dr Thompson's grand-daughter, is almost eight months old. Heather Mitchell is about to take Sunrise to a Pony Club Show Jumping Rally at Little Gaddesden.

Tracy had another part-bred Arab foal the following year and he was such a bright little chap that we named him Ashlyns Sunbird; he was born on the 29th February, 1976.

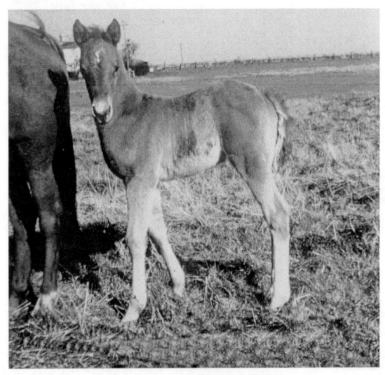

Ashlyns Sunbird at twenty days old

'Bird became a very successful jumper with Heather. They regularly competed on the annual sponsored Cross Country ride around the airfield at Halton on Sunbird. One year they were awarded a Gold Rosette for being one of the very few competitors who were able to jump not less than forty-eight of the fifty larger jumps on the lengthy course.

Sunbird at Halton Sponsored ride.

Another time they were jumping together in a Cross Country competition over a "Tiger Trap".

Sunbird at Tiger Trap, B.C.A. Cross Country, September 1982.

Summer 1983

Pictured here is Tracy with her two sons, Sunrise and Sunbird, taken in the summer of 1983. I am now aged sixty on Sunrise, Heather aged seventeen is in the middle on Sunbird and Alex, aged 6, is on the right on Tracy.

I understand from Mrs Mitchell that Sunbird still enjoys gentle hacks along the lovely bridleways on the Chiltern Hills.

June on Sunrise, August 1993

Sunrise and Sunbird have both given us great pleasure since the day they were foaled. We have enjoyed bringing them up and educating them so that they became our delightful friends with no nasty habits! Every rosette they subsequently won was a bonus.

Although Sunrise and Sunbird were full brothers their characters were quite different – we are sure Sunrise took after his father and wished we had had a chance to know Cochise better. If going out for a hack with a horse he had not met before Sunrise would arch his neck and strut about to show off. On subsequent meetings he would ignore it completely. He could be exasperating jumping for if he did not like the look of a fence he would determinedly stop and look at it. When he had satisfied himself that it was O.K. he would jump it without further fuss. It was hard to get a clear round on him!

Sunbird was always very careful and conscientious about what he did and was like his mother who was kind and generous – but did not like jumping.

After the annual Halton Cross Country they had both had a long day. Hacking to and from it as well as jumping fifty fences over a long course and hacking back again to the field. When they were checked last thing at night Sunrise would be happily relaxed and eating. 'Bird would still be reluctant to eat as he was still thinking over the events of the day.

When we moved to Berkhamsted Red was in a field near houses. In winter I used to go and feed him after work. Not wishing to disturb the nearby residents by calling out his name every evening, I trained Red to come to me when I whistled him in a certain way. I loved to hear galloping hooves in the darkness as he came for his food which he ate by the light of the street lamps. Years later I then taught Sunrise to come when I called him by whistling in the same way. This was particularly handy if he was grazing with other horses as he always had a head start on them before they realised what was happening and they also wanted to come into the stable for some of his goodies. This is when squabbling, biting or kicking could occur.

Although some horses become bossy and snappy if fed too many titbits this never happened with Sunrise no matter how many treats he had.

It was always safe to put a mint, or something even smaller, between my lips and he would take it with extreme gentleness. The only possible discomfort would be if I did it too often as his lips were rather bristly against mine.

Leslie, Sunrise and I retired to my home county of Lincolnshire in 1984.

Leslie and I have rarely ridden since retiring as we find the local rides so boring after all those years riding in the glorious beech woods in the Chilterns.

My friend June used to ride for miles on Sunrise exploring the local bridleways and reporting those which were closed or needed sign posting to the local authority who remedied this most successfully. In time Sunrise became bored as he had an excellent memory for every track June and he had travelled together. June stopped riding him in 2001 when he was twenty-six.

I fractured the neck of my femur in a riding accident in 1973 and was forbidden to ride for two years and the resultant arthritis made it difficult for me to mount from the ground. When out hacking with Sunrise I might occasionally drop my whip, hanky or glove. So I trained Sunrise to pick up the dropped article for me in his mouth and turn his head around so that I could take it from him without dismounting. This worked very well. I remember my hanky once blew onto a hedge and I had some difficulty in explaining to Sunrise that it was not on the ground but several feet up on a spiky hawthorn hedge. Happily he managed it for it was a cold and frosty day – just the sort when you need a hanky most of all. Needless to say I always kept my pockets well filled with rewards for when he was so helpful to me.

Sunrise also enjoyed helping to open or shut gates when we rode out together. He could hardly wait for me to open the sneck before he was ready to help push it open or slam it shut with his chest.

During the winter months June, Leslie and I would enjoy working on an ornamental wood which was planted for us in

1990 in an eleven acre field which was bequeathed to me by my half sister Elsie. Wild flower seed was sown with the grass seed when we turned it into our Nature Reserve instead of a ploughed arable field. A pond was dug in one corner and it is now one of the best sites for butterflies and dragonflies in the area.

Leslie and Sunrise riding around the young "Watts Wood" in 1994

On the morning of Sunday, 13th April, 2003 Sunrise was found to be ill from some unknown cause. I stayed with him all day whilst he was on painkillers and he seemed slightly better in the evening. However, at 8 p.m. his heart stopped beating and he gently slid to the straw beneath him. He had gone to join his mother Tracy and half-brother Sundown. It seems so strange without him. I have not even wanted to go into the stable now that he is no longer there. For Leslie and me it will always be filled with the ghost of Sunrise. We are going to plant a copper beech tree in the wood as a memorial to him.

Watts Wood – June, 2002. (Photo by Barry Hawthorn)

Watts Wood has grown well in the in the eight years since the photograph of Leslie and Sunrise in the young wood was taken.

I will now end my lengthy story which was originally intended to tell only of my five years in the WAAF.

I enjoyed being read to as a child; my favourite stories always ended with the words "and they both lived happily ever after."

Those same words are a fitting end to my book also. Thankfully they are true of us too. Leslie and I are still together. We are still happy.

19. *Fifty Years On – Morton Hall*

In 1988 my ex-WAAF colleague, Beryl Commin, came to stay with us and it was arranged that we could have a visit to our old haunts of Morton Hall. At that time it was a Semi Open Prison for Men. Our guide, Rosemary Arnold, was our escort for our wet afternoon visit. We were suitably impressed by the neat and attractive flower beds which lined the entrance driveway to where our Guard Room had once stood where we used to book in or out of Camp as necessary.

Driveway to Morton Hall – April 1988

Not far past the Guard Room there was a grassy paddock on the left where stood all the Nissen huts for WAAFs. None of these remained but here and there one could discern the concrete bases where they had once stood.

We then went to look for the Hall itself which I knew had been badly damaged by a mysterious fire a few years previously. Sadly all traces of it had been removed except for a few laurel bushes which still remained to indicate where it had once stood.

The only building from the past we saw was the large Nissen hut which had once been our NAAFI. It was now the church for the inmates.

Our former NAAFI – now the Church, April 1988

Here we are standing outside it. Rosemary Arnold on the left, then Sylvia, Beryl and Leslie. We were then taken by Rosemary to a Mess Room where one of the inmates brought us a cup of tea and biscuits. We chatted for a while hoping the rain would stop. We then left after our nostalgic visit to a place where we had both spent almost two years of our life which had, inevitably, left many memories still imprinted on our minds, both happy and sad. We were both in sombre mood when we left and the damp and drizzly weather matched our feelings.

In January, 2001 I was pleased to be told by the prison authorities that "In our training room we are shortly developing a history corner. It is our intention to ensure that the memory of the sacrifices made by all in the war years will live on, particularly with those with connections to 5 Group and Morton Hall."

Morton Hall is now a Secure Womens' Prison so has been surrounded by escape proof fencing and the only remnants which remain from the past are two gate pillars on the main entrance and part of the gymnasium. It now contains over 300 women prisoners so space is at a premium and it may well be that little will remain to tell of the past use when it was nerve centre of 5 Group Bomber Command.

In my previous book I told of my friendship with an Australian Navigator of 97 Squadron based at R.A.F. Woodhall Spa. After completing his first tour he went for a "rest" period of instructional duties to an O.T.U. at R.A.F. Upper Heyford on 12th March, 1943. This was followed by a posting to 1655 Mosquito Training Unit at R.A.F. Marham in Norfolk on 7th December, 1943. A month later he was being flown in a Mosquito by the very experienced pilot, F/Lt Jolly. Tragically their Mosquito exploded in mid-air and both men were killed. Two school children met at the site of the still smouldering wreckage and several years later were married. Mary and Stan celebrated their Golden Wedding in July, 2000.

Last summer we had the great pleasure of meeting Mary and Stan for the first time. They were brought up from Northampton to Lincoln by their friend Margaret, with whom they were staying. We were joined for lunch by Dawn and Colin Bowskill at a local hotel and had a very enjoyable and lengthy lunch. We hope to be able to do the same again this year.

Dawn, Stan, Sylvia and Mary (l to r) Luncheon party, Summer 2002

As a result of Stan telling a reporter of the Hereford Times about the Mosquito crash they published an article about it recently. This stirred the memory of Shirley Matthews who was a pupil at Glewstone School in the next village to Llangarron. She wrote to the "Hereford Times" saying that she "heard the scream of an aircraft engine" followed by an explosion. The entire class was evacuated into the back playground adjacent to a field. There the children watched two parachutes descending and "thousands of fragments of wood spiralling down". One pupil was to find a watch belonging to a flier which was passed on to the police. The flier's next of kin sent a letter of appreciation to the school which was read out by the headmistress.

Thanks to the efforts of the Rev Tony Kelk permission was obtained for a memorial plaque about the crash to be placed in Llangarron Church.

Brian Davies of the Hereford and The Marches Branch of the Air Crew Association has kindly made all the arrangements for me for a plaque to be made and suitably engraved and it is now in the church. A Dedication Service is being planned for Sunday, 12th October, 2003.

Dedication Plaque at Llangarron.

BOOK PROFTIS TO R.A.F. CHARITIES

All profits I can make from the sale of my two books about WAAF life will be given to R.A.F. charities. I am happy to report that due to the efforts of many people £500 has already been given to the Air Crew Association. A further £250 has gone to the volunteers who are restoring part of the old R.A.F. Woodhall Spa camp site where Roo was stationed when he was at the start of his tour of ops as a navigator of 97 Squadron before the Squadron went to 8 Group for Pathfinder duties.

This leaves us at present with £11.01 in the "kitty" until we sell some more books. Stan is doing very well at this in the Llangarron area having himself sold 40 copies!

FINALLY – I believe there is still a saying in use "Life Begins at Forty!" Don't be put off by this figure if you are older than this. If you feel you would like to record what life was like for you in this generation why not do so? Let your thoughts and feelings of NOW be handed down to your grandchildren or others of your family.

If there is something you want to accomplish do not wait until the saddest phrase of the English language "It's too late now" is indeed true. Take heart from me.

Here I am just finishing off the last page of my second – and final – book at the age of eighty!

Sylvia, July 2003

Sylvia's first book, *Tales of a Bomber Command WAAF* was published by Woodfield in 2002.

Also published by Woodfield...
The following titles are all available in high-quality softback format

RAF HUMOUR

Bawdy Ballads & Dirty Ditties of the RAF • A huge collection of the bawdy songs and rude recitations with which RAF personnel would entertain one-another in off-duty hours in WW2. Sure to amuse any RAF veteran. (uncensored – strictly adults only!) *"Not for the frail, the fraightfully posh or proper gels – but great fun for everyone else!"* **£9.95**

Upside Down Nothing on the Clock • Dozens of jokes and anecdotes contributed by RAF personnel from AC2s to the top brass... one of our best sellers. *"Highly enjoyable."* **£6.00**

Upside Down Again! • Our second great collection of RAF jokes, funny stories and anecdotes – a great gift for those with a high-flying sense of humour! *"Very funny indeed."* **£6.00**

Was It Like This For You? • A feast of humorous reminiscences & cartoons depicting the more comical aspects of life in the RAF. *"Will bring back many happy memories. Highly recommended."* **£6.00**

I Have Control • former RAF Parachute instructor **Edward Cartner** humorously recalls the many mishaps, blunders and faux-pas of his military career. *Superb writing; very amusing indeed.* **£9.95**

Who is in Charge Here...? • Former RAF Parachute instructor **Edward Cartner** regales us with more inglorious moments from the latter part of his military career as a senior officer. *Superb writing; very amusing indeed.* **£9.95**

MILITARY MEMOIRS & HISTORIES – THE POST-WAR PERIOD

A History of the King's Flight & The Queen's Flight • An illustrated history of the RAF's Royal illustrious squadron, responsible for the air transport of the Royal family from its inception in 1936 to its disbandment in 1995. **£15.00**

Flying the Waves • **Richard Pike** describes his eventful second career as a commercial helicepter pilot, which involved coastguard Air/Sea Rescue operations in the Shetlands and North Sea. **£9.95**

From Port T to RAF Gan • The history of the RAF's most deserted outpost is comprehensively and entertainingly charted by **Peter Doling**, a former RAF officer who served on Gan in the 1970s. Many photos, some in colour. **£20.00**

Korea: We Lived They Died • Former soldier with Duke of Wellington's Regt **Alan Carter** reveals the appalling truth of front-line life for British troops in this now forgotten war. *Very funny in places too.* **£9.95**

Meteor Eject! • Former 257 Sqn pilot [1950s] **Nick Carter** recalls the early days of RAF jets and his many adventures flying Meteors, including one very lucky escape via a Martin-Baker ejector seat... **£9.95**

Pluck Under Fire • Eventful Korean War experiences of **John Pluck** with the Middlesex Regiment. **£9.95**

Return to Gan • Michael Butler's light-hearted account of life at RAF Gan in 1960 and the founding of 'Radio Gan'. *Will delight those who also served at this remote RAF outpost in the Indian Ocean.* **£12.00**

The Spice of Flight • Former RAF pilot **Richard Pike** delivers a fascinating account of flying Lightnings, Phantoms and later helicopters with 56, 43(F) & 19 Sqns in the RAF of the 1960s & 70s. **£9.95**

Tread Lightly into Danger • Bomb-disposal expert **Anthony Charlwood**'s experiences in some of the world's most dangerous hotspots (Kuwait, Iraq, Lebanon, Somalia, etc) over the last 30 years. **£9.95**

MILITARY MEMOIRS & HISTORIES – WORLD WAR 1 & 2

A Bird Over Berlin Former Lancaster pilot with 61 Sqn **Tony Bird DFC** tells a remarkable tale of survival against the odds during raids on the German capital & as a POW. *"An incredible-but-true sequence of events."* **£9.95**

Algiers to Anzio with 72 & 111 Squadrons Former engineer officer **Greggs Farish**'s diary and photos are a superb historical record of RAF squadron life during Operation 'Husky' – the invasion of Sicily/Italy in 1943. **£9.95**

An Erk's-Eye View of World War 2 • former 'instrument basher' **Ted Mawdsley** salutes the work of the RAF ground crews of WW2, who played a vital role in keeping the RAF's aircraft flying in often adverse conditions. **£9.95**

An Illustrated History of RAF Waddington Former crewmember of the famous Battle of Britain flight Ray Leach has researched the wartime history of this important RAF base. Many photos. *"A superb achievement."* **£20.00**

A Lighter Shade of Blue • A former Radar Operator **Reg O'Neil** recalls his WW2 service in Malta and Italy with 16004 AMES – a front-line mobile radar unit. *'Interesting, informative and amusing.'* **£9.95**

A Shilling's Worth of Promises • Delightfully funny memoirs of **Fred Hitchcock,** recalling his years as an RAF airman during the war and later amusing escapades in the UK and Egypt. *A very entertaining read.* **£9.95**

Beaufighters BOAC & Me • WW2 Beaufighter navigator **Sam Wright** served a full tour with 254 Sqn and was later seconded to BOAC on early postwar overseas routes. *'Captures the spirit of the mighty Beaufighter'* **£9.95**

Carried on the Wind • **Sean Feast** tells the fascinating story of Ted Manners, a 'special duties operator' with 101 Squadron, whose job was to 'spoof' enemy radar and intercept their surface-to-air radio messages in WW2. **£9.95**

Coastal Command Pilot • Former Hudson pilot **Ted Rayner**'s outstanding account of his unusual WW2 Coastal Command experiences, flying in the Arctic from bases in Iceland and Greenland. **£9.95**

Cyril Wild: The Tall Man Who Never Slept • **James Bradley**'s biography of a remarkable Japanese-speaking British Army officer who helped many POWs survive at Sonkurai Camp on the infamous Burma railway. **£9.95**

Desert War Diary • **John Walton's** diary and photos record the activities of the Hurricanes and personnel of 213 Squadron during WW2 in Cyprus and Egypt. *"Informative and entertaining."* **£9.95**

Espionage Behind the Wire • former POW **Howard Greville** tells the fascinating story of how he worked as a spy for British intelligence (MI6) from inside a German POW camp. **£9.95**

From Fiji to Balkan Skies • Spitfire/Mustang pilot **Dennis McCaig** recalls eventful WW2 operations over the Adriatic/Balkans with 249 Sqn in 43/44. *'A rip-roaring real-life adventure, splendidly written.'* **£9.95**

Get Some In! • The many wartime adventures of **Mervyn Base**, a WW2 RAF Bomb Disposal expert **£9.95**

Hunt Like a Tiger • **Tom Docherty** an illustrated history of 230 squadron – equipped during the war with Sunderland flying boats which were put to many uses in many theatres of war. A fascinating piece of RAF history. **£9.95**

Just a Survivor • Former Lancaster navigator **Phil Potts** tells his remarkable tale of survival against the odds in the air with 103 Sqn and later as a POW. *'An enlightening and well written account.'* **£9.95**

Memoirs of a 'Goldfish' • The eventful wartime memoirs of former 115 Sqn Wellington pilot **Jim Burtt-Smith**, now president of the Goldfish Club - exclusively for aviators who have force-landed into water. **£9.95**

Nobody Unprepared • The history of No 78 Sqn RAF is told in full for the first time by **Vernon Holland** in this absorbing account of the Whitley/Halifax squadron's World War 2 exploits. Full statistics and roll of honour. **£14.95**

No Brylcreem, No Medals • RAF MT driver **Jack Hambleton** 's splendid account of his wartime escapades in England, Shetlands & Middle East blends comic/tragic aspects of war in uniquely entertaining way. **£9.95**

Nobody's Hero • Former RAF Policeman **Bernard Hart-Hallam**'s extraordinary adventures with 2TAF Security Section on D-Day and beyond in France, Belgium & Germany. *"Unique and frequently surprising."* **£9.95**

Operation Pharos • **Ken Rosam** tells the story of the RAF's secret bomber base/staging post on the Cocos Keeling islands during WW2 and of many operations from there. *'A fascinating slice of RAF history.'* **£9.95**

Over Hell & High Water • WW2 navigator **Les Parsons** survived 31 ops on Lancasters with 622 Sqn, then went on to fly Liberators in Far East with 99 Sqn. *'An exceptional tale of 'double jeopardy'.* **£9.95**

Pacifist to Glider Pilot • The son of Plymouth Brethren parents, **Alec Waldron** renounced their pacifism and went on to pilot gliders with the Glider Pilot Regiment at both Sicily & Arnhem. *Excellent photos.* **£9.95**

Pathfinder Force Balkans • Pathfinder F/Engineer **Geoff Curtis** saw action over Germany & Italy before baling out over Hungary. He was a POW in Komarno, Stalags 17a & 17b. *'An amazing catalogue of adventures.'* **£9.95**

Per Ardua Pro Patria • Humour and tragedy are interwoven in these unassuming autobiographical observations of **Dennis Wiltshire**, a former Lancaster Flight Engineer who later worked for NASA. **£9.95**

Ploughs, Planes & Palliasses • Entertaining recollections of RAF pilot **Percy Carruthers**, who flew Baltimores in Egypt with 223 Squadron and was later a POW at Stalag Luft 1 & 6. **£9.95**

RAF/UXB The Story of RAF Bomb Disposal • Stories contributed by wartime RAF BD veterans that will surprise and educate the uninitiated. *"Amazing stories of very brave men."* **£9.95**

Railway to Runway • Wartime diary & letters of Halifax Observer **Leslie Harris** – killed in action with 76 Sqn in 1943 – poignantly capture the spirit of the wartime RAF in the words of a 20-year-old airman. **£9.95**

Seletar Crowning Glory • The history of the RAF base in Singapore from its earliest beginnings, through the golden era of the flying-boats, its capture in WW2 and on to its closure in the 1970s. **£15.00**

The RAF & Me • Former Stirling navigator **Gordon Frost** recalls ops with 570 Sqn from RAF Harwell, including 'Market-Garden' 'Varsity' and others. *'A salute to the mighty Stirling and its valiant crews.'* **£9.95**

Training for Triumph • **Tom Docherty**'s very thorough account of the amazing achievement of RAF Training Command, who trained over 90,000 aircrew during World War 2. *'An impressively detailed book.'* **£12.00**

To Strive and Not to Yield • An inspiring account of the involvement of No 626 Squadron RAF Bomber Command in the 'Battle of Berlin' (1943/44) and a salute to the men and women who served on the squadron. **£14.95**

Un Grand Bordel • Geoffrey French relates air-gunner **Norman Lee**'s amazing real-life adventures with the French Maquis (Secret Army) after being shot down over Europe. *"Frequently funny and highly eventful."* **£9.95**

UXB Vol 2 • More unusual and gripping tales of bomb disposal in WW2 and after. **£9.95**

Wot! No Engines? • Alan Cooper tells the story of military gliders in general and the RAF glider pilots who served on Operation Varsity in 1945 in particular. A very large and impressive book with many photos. **£18.00**

While Others Slept • Former Hampden navigator **Eric Woods** tells the story of Bomber Command's early years and how he completed a tour of duty with 144 Squadron. *'Full of valuable historical detail.'* **£9.95**

WOMEN & WORLD WAR TWO

A WAAF at War • Former MT driver **Diana Lindo**'s charming evocation of life in the WAAF will bring back happy memories to all those who also served in World War 2. *"Nostalgic and good-natured."* **£9.95**

Corduroy Days • Warm-hearted and amusing recollections of **Josephine Duggan-Rees**'s wartime years spent as a Land Girl on farms in the New Forest area. *"Funny, nostalgic and very well written."* **£9.95**

Ernie • **Celia Savage**'s quest to discover the truth about the death of her father, an RAF Halifax navigator with 149 Sqn, who died in WW2 when she was just 6 years old. *"A real-life detective story."* **£9.95**

In My Father's Footsteps • **Pat Bienkowski**'s moving account of her trip to Singapore & Thailand to visit the places where her father and uncle were both POW's during WW2. **£9.95**

Lambs in Blue • **Rebecca Barnett's** revealing account of the wartime lives and loves of a group of WAAFs posted to the tropical paradise of Ceylon. *"A highly congenial WW2 chronicle."* **£9.95**

Radar Days • Delightful evocation of life in the wartime WAAF by former Radar Operator **Gwen Arnold**, who served at Bawdsey Manor RDF Station, Suffolk. *"Amusing, charming and affectionate."* **£9.95**

Searching in the Dark • The amusing wartime diary of **Peggy Butler** a WAAF radar operator 1942-1946 – written when she was just 19 yrs old and serving at Bawdsey RDF station in Suffolk **£9.95**

Tales of a Bomber Command Waaf (and her horse) • very entertaining book composed mainly of wartime letters received and sent by **Sylvia Pickering**, who served as a Waaf at RAF Cottesmore and RAF Coningsby. **£9.95**

More Tales of a Bomber Command Waaf (and her horse) • The second part of **Sylvia Pickering**'s war was spent at RAF Coningsby and HQ 5 Group (Bomber Command) at Morton Hall. Many more entertaining reminiscences. **£9.95**

Why Did We Join? • In this entertaining book **Eileen Smith** recalls the camaraderie, excitement and heartbreak of working as a Waaf on an operational Bomber Command Station – RAF East Kirkby in Lincolnshire. **£9.95**

MEMOIRS & HISTORIES – NON-MILITARY

A Beat Around the Bush • **Alastair Tompkins** recounts a variety of his extraordinary experiences– many of them very amusing indeed – as a Bush Policeman in British Colonial Kenya, 1952-62. Very entertaining. **£9.95**

20th CenturyFarmers Boy • Sussex farmer **Nick Adames** looks back on a century of rural change and what it has meant to his own family and the county they have farmed in for 400 years. **£9.95**

Call an Ambulance! • former ambulance driver **Alan Crosskill** recalls a number of light-hearted episodes from his eventful career in the 1960s/70s. *'Very amusing and entertaining'.* **£9.95**

Harry – An Evacuee's Story • The misadventures of **Harry Collins** – a young lad evacuated from his home in Stockport UK to Manitoba, Canada in WW2. *'An educational description of the life of an evacuee'* **£9.95**

Just Visiting • Charming and funny book by former Health Visitor **Molly Corbally**, who brilliantly depicts colourful characters and entertaining incidents from her long career. **£9.95**

Occupation Nurse • **Peter & Mary Birchenall** pay tribute to the achievement of the group of untrained nurses who provided healthcare at Guernsey's only hospital during the German occupation of 1940-45. **£9.95**

The JFK Assassination: Dispelling the Myths • Prepare to revise everything you thought you knew about the most famous assassination of the 20th Century. British historian **Mel Ayton** examines the many 'myths' that have grown up in the 40 years since JFK was murdered and debunks them all. You may be surprised at his conclusions. **£9.95**

FICTION

A Trace of Calcium by **David Barnett** • A commuter comes to the aid of a young woman in trouble, becomes implicated in murder and must use all his resources to clear his name. (contains sex & violence) **£9.95**

Double Time by **David Barnett** • A light-hearted time-travel fantasy in which a bookmaker tries to use a time machine to make his fortune and improve his love-life with hilarious consequences. (contains sex & violence) **£9.95**

Dust & Fury by **David Barnett** • An epic family saga set in the Sultanate of Oman, featuring the lives and loves of an Omani family during the bitter war that led to the foundation of modern Oman. (contains sex & violence) **£15.00**

The Brats • this very entertaining novel by **Tony Paul** is based on the true story of his grandfather, who as a boy along with several friends, stowed away on a ship bound for Canada. The youngsters' brutal mistreatment at the hands of the Captain and Mate of the ship caused a scandal that made headlines in Victorian times. **£9.95**

The Cherkassy Incident by **Hunter Carlyle** Terrorists plot to steal nuclear missiles from a sunken Russian nuclear submarine; can an international team of security agents stop them? (contains sex & violence) **£9.95**

BOOKS FEATURING THE SOUTH COAST & THE SOUTH DOWNS REGION

A Portrait of Slindon • **Josephine Duggan Rees** has written a charming history of this attractive and well-preserved West Sussex village, from its earliest beginnings to the present day, taking in the exploits of its many notable residents over the years. Very informative and entertaining. Illustrated with many photos, some in colour. **£14.95**

Retribution • **Mike Jupp** has created an outrageous and very funny comedy/fantasy novel for adults and older children, featuring bizarre goings-on in a fictional quiet English seaside town that bears a striking resemblance to Mike's home town of Bognor Regis. Brilliantly illustrated. *One of the funniest books you will ever read.* **£9.95**

Unknown to History and Fame • **Brenda Dixon**'s charming portrait of Victorian life in the West Sussex village of Walberton via the writings of Charles Ayling, a resident of the village, whose reports on local events were a popular feature in *The West Sussex Gazette* over many years during the Victorian era. **£9.95**

A Little School on the Downs • **Mary Bowmaker** tells the amazing story of Harriet Finlay-Johnson, headmistress of a little village school in Sompting, West Sussex in the 1890s, whose ideas and classroom techniques began a revolution in education. She also scandalised society at the time by marrying a former pupil, 20 years her junior. **£9.95**

The South Coast Beat Scene of the 1960s The South Coast may not have been as famous as Liverpool in the swinging sixties but it was nevertheless a hotbed of musical activity. Broadcaster **Mike Read** traces the complete history of the musicians, the fans and the venues from Brighton to Bognor in this large and lavishly-illustrated book. **£24.95**

Boys & Other Animals • **Josephine Duggan Rees's** warm-hearted and delightfully funny account of a mother's many trials and tribulations bringing up a boisterous all-male family on a farm in rural Sussex during the 1950s-70s. **£9.95**